The Usborne
Children's
Cookbook

Rebecca Gilpin

Designed by Non Figg and Nancy Leschnikoff
Illustrated by Molly Sage and Adam Larkum

Photography by Howard Allman
Recipes and food preparation by Catherine Atkinson

Contents

Using this book

The delicious recipes in this book are ideal for anyone who is just starting out in the kitchen. The recipes are explained in a clear, simple way, without baffling cooking terms and jargon. As well as the recipes, there are general pages which show you how to cook things such as rice, potatoes and bread rolls. You'll also find helpful chefs who give you cooking tips and hints. So, read this page, then get cooking!

Getting ready

Before you start, check that you've got all the ingredients that are in the list at the beginning of the recipe. Read through the recipe too, to make sure that you have all the equipment you will need.

The right amount

When you add a spoonful of something to a mixture, the ingredient should lie level with the top of the spoon and not heaped up. Measuring spoons found in a set are the easiest to use, but if you don't have any, use ordinary spoons.

A set of measuring spoons

Cooking times

Not all ovens are the same and some cook things more quickly or slowly. Check to see if the food is cooked, close to the cooking time in the recipe.

A level spoonful of chilli powder

Find out about different herbs and spices on pages 40-41.

Salt and pepper

In the recipes, salt and pepper are added a pinch at a time. A 'pinch' is the amount you can pick up between your first finger and thumb. Don't add more than it says – you can add extra when you eat the food.

Hot ovens

When you're cooking something in an oven, put it on the middle shelf unless the recipe says something else. Fan ovens are hotter than other ovens, so check in the instruction book to see if you need to lower the temperature or cook something for less time.

Serving suggestions

Some of the recipes in this book are complete meals in themselves. Other recipes have suggestions for things which could be served with them. If you want to serve something with potatoes, rice or a salad, look in the index at the back of the book.

Greek salad

Greek salad is great as a summer lunch, served with fresh crusty bread. It contains feta, a white salty Greek cheese, as well as cucumber, tomatoes, onions and olives.

Ingredients:

Serves 4

half a cucumber
450g (1lb) ripe tomatoes
1 red onion
200g (7oz) packet of feta
    cheese
75g (3oz) stoned black or
    green olives, drained

For the dressing:
1 garlic clove
4 tablespoons olive oil
1 tablespoon white wine vinegar
half a teaspoon of fresh, or
    quarter of a teaspoon of
    dried oregano
a pinch of caster sugar
salt and ground black pepper

Chef's Tip

Olives can be very salty. If you want to make them less salty, soak them in cold water for an hour, then drain them through a colander.

1. Cut the ends off the cucumber, then cut it in half along its length. Lay each half with the flat side facing down. Then, cut both halves into thin slices.

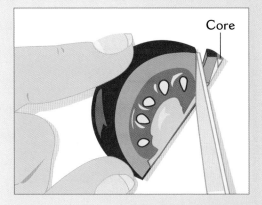

Core

2. Cut the tomatoes into quarters. Then, carefully cut out the central core of each one and throw it away. Put the tomato quarters and cucumber slices into a large bowl.

3. Cut the ends off the onion. Peel it and cut it into quarters, then cut the quarters into slices. Then, open the packet of feta cheese and pour away any liquid.

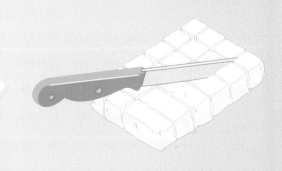

4. Cut the feta cheese into cubes, then add it to the bowl. Add the slices of onion and most of the olives. Mix everything together with your hands.

You need to use a jar with a lid.

5. Peel and crush the garlic. Put the olive oil, vinegar, garlic, oregano and sugar into a jam jar. Add a pinch of salt and of pepper, then screw the lid on tightly.

6. Shake the jar well to mix the dressing. Drizzle the dressing over the salad, then mix it with your hands. Then, scatter the rest of the olives over the top.

Couscous salad

Couscous is often eaten with grilled meat, fish or vegetables. It can also be mixed with other ingredients to make a salad. This recipe has a fresh lemon juice dressing.

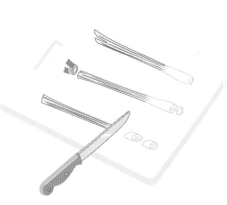

Ingredients:

Serves 4

8 spring onions
half a vegetable stock cube
1 tablespoon sunflower oil
225g (8oz) couscous
4 ripe tomatoes
half a cucumber
1 yellow pepper
4 tablespoons chopped fresh mint

For the dressing:
2 tablespoons sunflower oil
2 tablespoons fresh lemon juice
salt and ground black pepper

1. Using a sharp knife, cut off the ends of the spring onions and remove the outer layer. Then, cut the onions into diagonal slices about 1cm (½in) wide.

2. Put the half stock cube into a heatproof jug. Then, pour in 225ml (8 fl oz) of boiling water and stir it until the stock cube has completely dissolved.

Use a medium heat.

3. Put one tablespoon of oil in a large saucepan and add the onions. Heat the pan for 30 seconds, then pour in the stock. Cook the mixture until the liquid boils.

4. Remove the pan from the heat and add the couscous. Stir it in with a wooden spoon. Then, cover the pan with a lid and leave it for three minutes.

Chef's Tip

Vegetable stock is used to add flavour to recipes, but it's not a problem here if you don't have any. You can cook the couscous in boiling water instead.

5. If there is still any liquid in the pan, gently heat it over a low heat for a few minutes, until all the liquid is absorbed. Keep stirring the couscous to stop it from sticking.

6. For the dressing, put two tablespoons of oil in a small bowl. Add the lemon juice and a pinch of salt and of pepper and mix everything with a fork.

Throw away the seeds and core.

You don't need the seeds.

7. Spoon the couscous into a large bowl. While it is still warm, pour the dressing over it. Use a fork to break up any lumps, then leave the couscous to cool.

8. Cut the tomatoes in half and then in half again. Scoop out the seeds with a teaspoon. Then, cut out the green core and cut the tomatoes into small pieces.

9. Cut the ends off the cucumber and cut it in half, lengthways. Scoop out the seeds, then cut each half into long strips. Then, cut each strip into small pieces.

You could serve the couscous on some mixed salad leaves.

10. Cut the ends off the yellow pepper and cut it in half. Remove the seeds and cut the pepper into small pieces. Then, mix the mint and vegetables into the couscous.

7

Potato salad and green salad

Potatoes can be eaten hot or cold. This potato salad can be eaten while it's still warm but is also good served chilled, with a crunchy green salad and lamb kebabs (see pages 58-59).

Ingredients:

Serves 4

675g (1½lb) equal-sized new potatoes
salt
4 spring onions

For the dressing:
3 tablespoons mayonnaise
3 tablespoons Greek or plain natural yogurt
1 teaspoon fresh lemon juice
1 teaspoon wholegrain mustard
2 tablespoons chopped fresh dill
a pinch of freshly ground black pepper

For the green salad:
2 little gem lettuces, or a cos lettuce
half a cucumber
1 green pepper

Chef's Tip

If some of your new potatoes are much bigger than the others, cut them in half. All the pieces need to be about the same size, so that they cook in the same time.

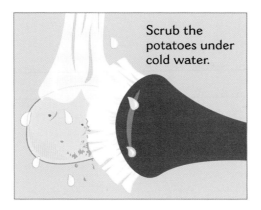

Scrub the potatoes under cold water.

1. Scrub the potatoes clean with a soft brush. Then, half-fill a large saucepan with water and add two pinches of salt. Heat the water until it boils.

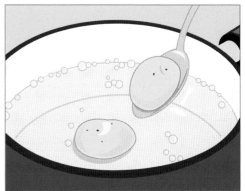

2. Put the potatoes into the pan. Heat the water until it boils, then reduce the heat a little, so that the water is gently bubbling. Cook the potatoes for 15-20 minutes.

3. While the potatoes are cooking, put all the ingredients for the dressing into a small bowl. Then, stir them with a spoon until they are mixed together.

4. Put a colander in the sink and carefully pour the cooked potatoes into it. Shake the colander a little, to drain off any extra water. Then, leave the potatoes to cool a little.

5. Using a sharp knife, cut off the ends of the spring onions, and remove the outer layer. Then, cut across the onions to make lots of thin slices, like this.

6. When the potatoes are cool enough to handle, put them on a chopping board and cut them into bite-sized pieces. Then, put all the pieces into a large bowl.

Take out the seeds, too.

7. Spoon the dressing over the potatoes while they are still slightly warm. Add the slices of spring onion and mix everything together with a large spoon.

You could dress the green salad with French dressing (see steps 11 and 12 on page 17).

8. For the green salad, cut off the bottom of each lettuce. Remove the leaves, wash them and shake them dry. Then, cut the ends off the pepper and finely slice it.

9. Cut the ends off the cucumber, then cut it in half, lengthways. Cut each half into lots of thin slices, then put the lettuce, pepper and cucumber into a large bowl.

Let the potato salad cool completely and keep it in the fridge until you're ready to eat it.

Sprinkle chopped spring onions on top and add a sprig of dill.

9

Leek and potato soup

This soup can make a warming meal on a winter day, but it's also delicious cold. The recipe uses a food processor, but if you cut the vegetables into very small pieces, you can make a chunky soup instead. If you've never prepared leeks before, look at page 53 before you start.

Ingredients:

Serves 4

3 leeks
1 onion
40g (1½oz) butter
350g (12oz) potatoes
1 vegetable stock cube
1 bay leaf
salt and ground black pepper
300ml (½ pint) milk

Chef's Tip

If you pour hot soup straight from the pan into a bowl, you may get splashed. It's much safer to spoon the soup into the bowl using a ladle.

1. Trim the leeks, then cut them into thin slices. Cut the ends off the onion and peel it. Cut it in half, slice it and cut it into small pieces. Put the butter into a large pan.

Steam escapes through the gap.

2. Gently heat the butter until it melts. Add the leeks and onion and stir them in, to coat them with melted butter. Put a lid on the pan, leaving a small gap.

Put the lid back on when you've stirred the soup.

3. Cook the leeks and onion on a low heat for 8-10 minutes, stirring them every now and then, with a wooden spoon. When they are soft, switch off the heat.

4. Peel the potatoes and cut them in half. Cut the halves into slices and cut the slices into small chunks. Then, put the stock cube in a heatproof jug.

5. Pour 600ml (1 pint) of boiling water into the jug and stir it until the stock cube has dissolved. Then, add the stock and the chunks of potato to the pan.

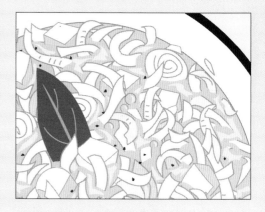

6. Add the bay leaf and a pinch of salt and of pepper. Heat the soup until it boils, then turn down the heat, so that it is gently bubbling. Cover the pan with a lid, as before.

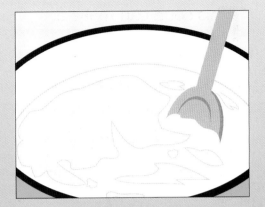

7. Cook the soup for 15-20 minutes, or until the potatoes are soft. Turn off the heat and remove the bay leaf with a spoon. Then, let the soup cool for 15 minutes.

8. Ladle half of the soup into a food processor and blend it until it is smooth. Spoon it into a large bowl, then blend the rest. Pour all of the soup back into the pan.

9. Add the milk and stir it in. For hot soup, gently re-heat the soup until it is just starting to bubble. Alternatively, for cold soup, put the soup in a fridge to chill.

Stir a spoonful of crème fraîche into the top of each bowl and sprinkle chopped chives over the top.

Spicy bean soup

This soup is hot and spicy. If you'd like it to be less spicy, just add the coriander and cumin and leave out the chilli.

Ingredients:

Serves 4

1 red onion
1 tablespoon olive oil
1 vegetable stock cube
1 clove of garlic
half a teaspoon of mild chilli
    powder
half a teaspoon of ground
    coriander
half a teaspoon of ground cumin
450ml (¾ pint) tomato juice
salt and ground black pepper
400g (14oz) can of red kidney
    beans or mixed beans
1 tablespoon chopped fresh
    coriander or parsley

1. Peel the onion and cut it in half. Finely slice it, then cut all of the slices into small pieces. Put the pieces of onion into a large saucepan with the olive oil.

2. Heat the pan on a low heat and gently cook the onion for 6-10 minutes, until it is soft. Stir the onion frequently, to stop it sticking to the pan.

You could sprinkle each bowl with chopped fresh coriander or parsley.

If you want to make bread rolls to eat with your soup, see pages 74-75.

3. While the onion is cooking, put the stock cube into a heatproof jug. Carefully pour 450ml (¾ pint) of boiling water into the jug and stir it until the cube dissolves.

4. Take the pan off the heat. Peel and crush the garlic and add it to the pan. Then, add the chilli powder, ground coriander and ground cumin, too.

5. Stir everything in the pan together. Then, heat the pan gently for one minute, stirring all the time, to stop the spices sticking as they cook.

Chef's Tip

6. Pour the tomato juice and stock into the pan and add a pinch of salt and of pepper. Open the can of beans and pour them into a colander in the sink.

Cans of beans usually contain a sugary liquid, as well as the beans. To rinse off the liquid, hold the colander under cold running water and gently shake the beans.

7. Add the rinsed beans to the pan. Stir the soup well and heat it until it boils. Then, reduce the heat a little, so that the soup is gently bubbling.

Steam escapes through the gap.

Scoop up lots of beans with the ladle, too.

8. Put the lid on the pan, leaving a small gap. Cook the soup for 15 minutes, stirring it from time to time. Then, turn off the heat and let the soup cool for 15 minutes.

9. Using a ladle, put half of the soup into a food processor and blend it until it is smooth and thick. Then, ladle the blended soup back into the pan.

10. Stir all of the soup in the pan together, then heat it until it is gently bubbling. Stir in the chopped coriander or parsley, then serve the soup.

Eggs

Eggs are used in many recipes, but they can also be cooked on their own. On these pages, you can find out how to prepare them for use in recipes, and how to boil, hard-boil and fry them.

Separate bowls

Make sure that the eggs you're using are fresh. In case they're not, it's a good idea to break them into a separate bowl or mug before you add them to a mixture. This means that you can throw away an egg that has gone off without having to throw everything else away too. In some recipes you may need only the egg white or yolk, so you'll need to separate the egg (see below).

Break eggs into a separate bowl, cup or mug before adding them to a mixture (see left).

Breaking an egg

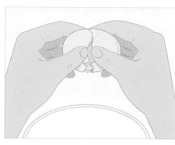

1. Unless you're boiling an egg, you'll need to break its shell. Crack the shell, by tapping it sharply on the edge of a bowl or mug.

2. Push your thumbs into the crack and pull the shell apart. Slide the egg into the bowl or mug and check for pieces of shell.

Separating

Break an egg onto a plate. Cover the yolk with an egg cup, then hold the egg cup and tip the plate. The egg white slides off.

Beating

When you beat an egg, you need to mix the yolk and the white of the egg evenly. Use a fork to mix them together.

Whisking egg whites

The tea towel helps to stop the bowl slipping.

Use a clean whisk.

1. Separate the eggs, then pour the whites into a clean, dry bowl. Place the bowl on a damp tea towel, then tilt the bowl.

2. Using your other hand, twist a whisk around and around very quickly in the bowl. The egg will begin to go white and frothy.

3. Carry on whisking the eggs until stiff points or 'peaks' form on the top when you lift up the whisk, like this.

Boiling an egg

For a solid yolk, cook the egg for longer.

Heat a pan of water until the water is boiling. Then, put an egg into the pan, using a spoon. Boil the egg for four minutes.

These are brown and
white hens' eggs.

This egg has
been hard-boiled
and peeled (see
page 17).

Quails' eggs are very
small and need to be
cooked for only two
minutes. To hard-boil
them, cook them for
four minutes.

Hard-boiling

Frying

Spooning hot oil over the
yolk helps it to cook.

For a hard-boiled egg,
boil the egg for 10
minutes, then lift it out
and place it in a bowl of
cold water, to cool.

1. Pour a tablespoon of
vegetable oil into a frying
pan. Heat the pan over a
medium heat for a minute,
then take it off the heat.

2. Crack an egg, then
hold it just above the pan
and open the shell. Tip
the egg into the oil, then
put the pan on the heat.

3. When the egg white
starts to turn solid, spoon
hot oil over the yolk. Fry
the egg for 3-4 minutes,
until it is cooked.

Salade niçoise

This salad is delicious and filling. It was first made in Nice, in the south of France, using local ingredients such as olives, anchovies and tuna.

Ingredients:

Serves 4

2 medium eggs
350g (12oz) small new potatoes
225g (8oz) thin green beans
2 little gem lettuces, or a cos lettuce
1 red onion
half a cucumber
16 ripe baby tomatoes
50g (2oz) can of anchovies
200g (7oz) can of tuna in oil
12 stoned black olives
2 teaspoons capers

For the French dressing:
4 tablespoons olive oil
1 tablespoon balsamic vinegar, or red wine vinegar
half a teaspoon of Dijon mustard
salt and ground black pepper

1. Hard-boil the eggs. Then, scrub the potatoes clean with a soft brush, under cold water. Half-fill a large saucepan with water and heat it until the water boils.

2. Using a spoon, put the potatoes in the pan. Heat the water until it boils. Reduce the heat a little so that the water is gently bubbling. Cook the potatoes for 10 minutes.

Use clean kitchen scissors.

3. While the potatoes cook, cut off the ends of the beans, then cut them in half. When the potatoes have been cooking for 10 minutes, add the beans to the pan.

4. Bring the water back to the boil and cook the potatoes and beans for five minutes. Put a colander into the sink and carefully pour the vegetables into it.

You could serve the salad with freshly-baked bread rolls (see pages 74-75).

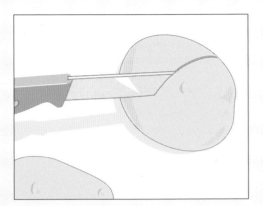

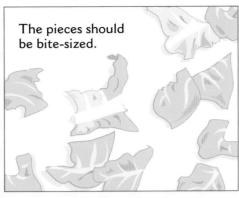
The pieces should be bite-sized.

5. When the potatoes are cool enough to handle, cut each one in half. Then, put the potatoes and beans in a large bowl and leave them to cool.

6. Cut off the bottom of the lettuce. Remove the leaves and wash them well in cold water. Shake them dry, then break the leaves into pieces.

7. Cut the ends off the onion and peel it. Then, cut it into halves and slice it. Cut off the ends of the cucumber, then cut it into slices. Then, cut the tomatoes in half.

Chef's Tip

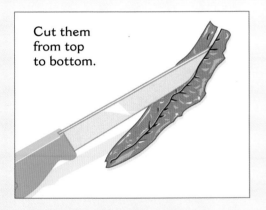
Cut them from top to bottom.

Don't rinse the tuna.

8. Carefully open the can of anchovies and tip them into a sieve. They are very salty, so rinse them under a cold tap. Then, cut each one in half.

9. Open the can of tuna and drain off the oil. Break it into large chunks. Add it to the bowl, with the anchovies, cucumber, lettuce, onion and tomatoes.

In the next step, you'll be peeling the shells off the hard-boiled eggs. Tap each egg gently on a plate until the shell cracks all the way around, then peel off the pieces.

Cut the eggs lengthways.

10. Peel the shells off the eggs and cut each egg into quarters. Then, drain the olives through a sieve. Spoon the capers into the sieve and drain them too.

11. Add the eggs, olives and capers to the bowl. Then, for the dressing, put the olive oil, vinegar, mustard and a pinch of salt and of pepper into a jar with a lid.

12. Screw the lid onto the jar, then shake the jar to mix the ingredients. Pour the dressing over the salad. Mix everything well with a large spoon.

Spanish omelette

This tasty vegetarian omelette is packed with vegetables. It is light and fluffy, but filling, too. Some omelettes are cooked in a frying pan, but this one is baked in the oven. It can be eaten straight away or when it has cooled.

Ingredients:

Serves 4

1 onion
2 medium-sized potatoes
1 courgette
1 clove of garlic
2 tablespoons olive oil
15g (½oz) butter
5 medium eggs
150ml (¼ pint) milk
half a teaspoon of mixed herbs
salt and ground black pepper

a shallow 20-23cm (8-9in) ovenproof dish

1. Heat the oven to 180°C, 350°F, gas mark 4. While it is heating up, wipe a paper towel in a little butter, then wipe butter over the inside of the dish.

2. Cut the ends off the onion and peel it. Cut it in half, then into thin slices. Then, peel the potatoes and cut them in half. Cut them into thin slices and then into cubes.

Stir the onion and potatoes now and then.

3. Cut the ends off the courgette and cut it in half lengthways. Cut the halves into strips and cut the strips into small pieces. Then, peel the clove of garlic.

4. Put the oil and butter into a non-stick frying pan. Heat them over a low heat until the butter melts. Add the onion and potatoes and cook them for five minutes.

Stir the vegetables often.

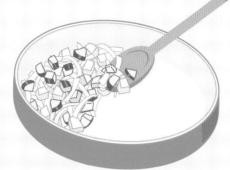

5. Add the pieces of courgette and crush the garlic into the pan. Cook everything gently for another five minutes, or until the vegetables are slightly soft.

6. Take the pan off the heat and spoon the vegetables into the ovenproof dish. Spread them out to make an even layer. Then, break the eggs into a large bowl.

7. Beat the eggs with a fork, then pour in the milk. Add the herbs and a pinch of salt and of pepper. Then, beat everything together until they are mixed well.

The omelette is delicious served with mixed salad leaves or a green salad like the one on pages 8-9.

8. Pour the egg mixture over the vegetables. Then, put the dish into the oven and bake the omelette for 40 minutes, until it is set and golden brown.

Lift out the pieces with a fish slice or pie slice.

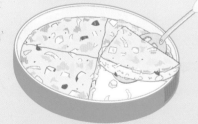

9. Push a knife into the middle of the omelette. If runny egg comes out, cook it for 5-10 minutes more. Then, run a knife around the edge and cut the omelette into pieces.

Croque-monsieur

This hot sandwich is perfect on its own as a light meal, or delicious served with a crunchy mixed salad.

Ingredients:

Serves 4

100g (4oz) Cheddar cheese
8 slices of medium-thickness bread
50g (2oz) butter, softened
4 slices of lean ham
2 teaspoons sunflower oil

For the mixed salad:
1 little gem lettuce, or half a cos lettuce
half a cucumber
1 carrot

Sprinkle the cheese as evenly as you can.

1. Lay four of the slices of bread on a chopping board. Spread a thin layer of butter on one side of each one. Then, butter the other four slices of bread in the same way.

2. Grate the cheese on the big holes on a grater. Then, sprinkle the grated cheese over four of the slices of buttered bread and lay a slice of ham on the top.

You could make the French dressing on pages 16-17 and sprinkle it over the salad.

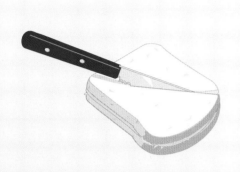

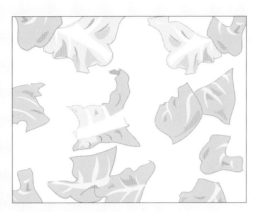

3. Gently press a slice of bread on top of each slice of ham. Cut each sandwich in half with a sharp knife, then put them on a plate and cover them with plastic foodwrap.

4. For the salad, cut the bottom off the lettuce. Pull off the leaves, rinse them in cold water and shake them dry. Tear them into bite-sized pieces and put them into a bowl.

5. Cut the ends off the cucumber. Then, cut the cucumber in half, lengthways, and in half again. Cut the pieces into small chunks, then add them to the bowl.

6. Peel the carrot with a potato peeler. Then, hold it firmly and carefully grate it on the biggest holes on a grater. Add the carrot to the bowl and mix everything well.

7. Put one teaspoon of the sunflower oil into a large, non-stick frying pan. Then, heat the oil over a medium heat for about a minute.

Chef's Tip

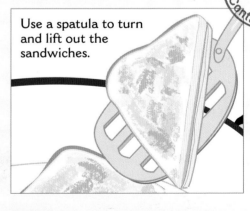

Use a spatula to turn and lift out the sandwiches.

8. Carefully put four of the half sandwiches into the frying pan. Cook them for 2-3 minutes, or until their undersides have turned brown and crisp.

When you fry things in a pan, they can cook very quickly. To see if the sandwiches are cooked, slide a spatula under a corner of one of them and have a look.

9. Turn the sandwiches over. Cook them for 2-3 minutes, then lift them out of the pan. Add another teaspoon of oil to the pan and cook the remaining sandwiches.

Beefburgers with tomato salsa

These tasty beefburgers are baked in the oven. They are delicious served with fresh tomato salsa and chunky potato wedges (see page 65).

Ingredients:

Serves 4

For the tomato salsa:
6 ripe tomatoes
1 red onion
2 tablespoons chopped fresh coriander
1 tablespoon olive oil
1 teaspoon balsamic vinegar or red wine vinegar
salt and ground black pepper

For the burgers:
1 tablespoon olive oil
1 teaspoon dried mixed herbs
2 teaspoons soy sauce or Worcestershire sauce
1 slice of medium-thickness white bread, with the crusts removed
1 medium egg
450g (1lb) lean minced beef
salt and ground black pepper

1. Heat the oven to 200°C, 400°F, gas mark 6. Then, put a teaspoon of cooking oil on a baking tray. Wipe the oil over the tray with a paper towel.

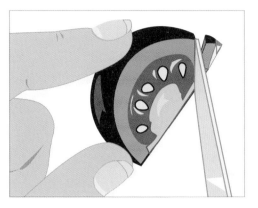

2. For the salsa, cut each tomato in half, then into quarters. Cut out the core of each one, like this. Throw away the cores, then cut all the quarters into small pieces.

Keep the other half of the onion for the burgers.

3. Peel the onion and chop it finely. Put half of it into a bowl with the tomatoes and add the chopped coriander, olive oil, vinegar and a pinch of salt and of pepper.

4. Stir everything in the bowl together, then put the salsa on one side. Then, put the rest of the onion into a frying pan with a tablespoon of olive oil.

Chef's Tip

5. Cook the onion over a low heat for 8-10 minutes, stirring it frequently to stop it sticking to the pan. When the onion is soft, take the pan off the heat.

6. Spoon the onion into a large bowl. Stir in the dried mixed herbs and soy or Worcestershire sauce and leave the mixture to cool for about 10 minutes.

In the next step, you'll be making breadcrumbs in a food processor. If you don't have one, grate some bread on the big holes on a grater. Slightly stale bread works best.

Use clean hands to mix the ingredients.

Leave spaces between the burgers.

7. Make the slices of bread into breadcrumbs, using a food processor (see page 94) or a grater. Then, break the egg into a small bowl and beat it with a fork.

8. Add the breadcrumbs, egg, beef and a pinch of salt and of pepper to the large bowl. Break up the beef with a wooden spoon, then mix all the ingredients together well.

9. Divide the mixture into four pieces. Make each piece into a circle about 1cm (½in) thick. Then, put the burgers on the greased baking tray.

Turn the burgers with a fish slice.

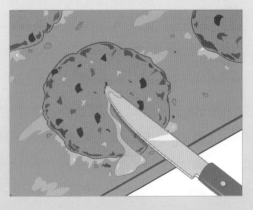

10. Cook the burgers in the oven for 10 minutes. Then, lift them out, wearing oven gloves. Turn them over and cook them for another 10 minutes.

11. To check that the burgers are cooked through, push a knife into them, then press on the top. The juices which run out should be clear, not pink.

Pastry

On these pages, you can find out how to make shortcrust pastry, which is used to make flans, pies and quiches (see pages 26-27). You'll also find out how to 'blind' bake a pastry case, before filling it. It's much easier to make pastry if your hands are cool, but once you've made it, try not to handle it too much.

'Blind' baking

When a pastry case is 'blind' baked, it is cooked for a time with no filling. It is lined with kitchen foil and filled with ceramic baking beans, or dried beans or peas, which stop the pastry bubbling up in the middle.

If you use dried beans or peas when you're baking pastry, store them in an airtight jar, so that you can use them again and again.

Ingredients:

Makes enough pastry to line a 20cm (8in) flan tin

175g (6oz) plain flour
salt
75g (3oz) butter, or
    margarine from a block
2-3 tablespoons cold
    water

baking beans, or a packet
    of dried beans or peas

1. Sift the flour and a pinch of salt through a sieve into a large bowl. Then, cut the butter into cubes and stir them in.

2. Rub the butter into the flour with the tips of your fingers. Carry on rubbing until the mixture looks like fine breadcrumbs.

Use a blunt knife.

3. Sprinkle two tablespoons of cold water over the mixture. Then, stir it in, until everything starts to stick together.

This pastry has been rolled out, which means that it has been rolled flat with a rolling pin.

4. If the pastry feels dry, mix in another tablespoon of water. Then, squeeze the pastry against the side of the bowl.

5. Sprinkle a little flour on a clean work surface. Then, lift the pastry onto the surface and pat it into a smooth ball.

6. Wrap the pastry in plastic foodwrap. Then, put it into a fridge for 20 minutes. This makes it easier to roll out flat.

Ceramic baking beans, like these, can usually be bought in the cookery department of any large store.

Lining a pastry case

Turn the pastry a quarter of the way around.

1. Put the pastry onto a floury surface. Sprinkle flour on a rolling pin. Roll over the pastry once, then turn it.

2. Roll over and turn the pastry again and again. Carry on until the pastry is slightly bigger than the flan tin.

Be careful not to make any holes in the pastry.

3. Roll the pastry around the rolling pin. Lift it up and unroll it over the tin. Gently push the pastry into the edges of the tin.

The rolling pin cuts off any extra pastry.

4. Roll the rolling pin over the tin. Then, cover the pastry case with plastic foodwrap and put it in a fridge for 20 minutes.

'Blind' baking

The holes stop the pastry rising up.

1. Put a baking sheet in the oven. Heat the oven to 200°C, 400°F, gas mark 6. Then, prick the pastry base with a fork.

Try not to squash the pastry.

2. Cut a large square of kitchen foil and gently press it into the pastry case. Then, fill the foil with baking beans.

3. Lift out the hot baking sheet and put the flan tin on it. Put it back into the oven and bake the pastry case for 10 minutes.

4. Carefully remove the hot foil and beans. Then, bake the empty case for another 8-10 minutes, or until it is pale golden.

Bacon and onion quiche

To make the pastry base for this tasty quiche, you'll need to follow the steps on pages 24-25. When you've 'blind' baked the base, you can make the filling for the quiche.

Ingredients:

Serves 4

For the pastry:
175g (6oz) plain flour
salt
75g (3oz) butter or margarine
   from a block
2-3 tablespoons cold water

For the filling:
6 rashers of unsmoked bacon
1 onion
1 tablespoon sunflower oil
100g (4oz) Cheddar cheese
2 medium eggs
150ml (¼ pint) milk
ground black pepper

baking beans or a packet of dried
   peas or beans, for 'blind' baking
a 20cm (8in) flan tin, about
   3.5cm (1½in) deep

Be very careful when you remove the hot foil and beans.

The hot baking sheet helps the bottom of the quiche to cook.

1. To make the pastry, follow the steps on pages 24-25. Line the tin with the pastry, then 'blind' bake the pastry case. When it is cooked, take it out of the oven.

2. Put the hot baking sheet back into the oven on its own. Reduce the temperature of the oven to 170°C, 325°F, gas mark 3. Then, prepare the filling for the quiche.

3. If there is any rind on the bacon, cut it off with clean kitchen scissors and throw the rind away. Then, cut the rest of the bacon into small pieces.

4. Peel the onion and cut it in half. Slice it, then cut it into small pieces. Put the pieces into a frying pan with the oil and cook them gently for about five minutes.

5. Add the bacon to the pan and stir it in. Then, turn off the heat and tip the pieces of bacon and onion into a bowl. Let them cool for five minutes.

The quiche can be eaten hot, but it is also delicious chilled. Make sure it is completely cool before you put it in the fridge.

6. Grate the cheese on the large holes on a grater and sprinkle half of it over the bottom of the pastry case. Then, scatter the bacon and onion over the top.

7. Sprinkle over the rest of the cheese. Break the eggs into a small bowl and mix them with a fork. Pour the milk into a jug and mix in the egg and a pinch of pepper.

The top should be golden and the middle set firm.

8. Slowly pour the egg mixture over the filling in the pastry case. Then, carefully lift the hot baking sheet out of the oven and put the quiche onto it.

9. Bake the quiche for about 20-30 minutes, then push a knife into the middle. If it isn't firm, cook it for 5-10 minutes more. Leave it in the tin for 10 minutes before serving it.

27

Pizza

This pizza has a light bread base, topped with a tasty tomato sauce and grated mozzarella. It takes a little while to make the base, but it's delicious.

Ingredients:

Serves 4

For the base:
225g (8oz) strong white bread
   flour
half a teaspoon of salt
1 teaspoon dried easy-blend yeast
150ml (¼ pint) warm water,
   which has been boiled
1 tablespoon olive oil

For the tomato sauce:
two cloves of garlic
1 tablespoon olive oil
400g (14oz) can chopped
   tomatoes
a pinch of caster sugar
half a teaspoon of dried oregano
   or mixed dried herbs
salt and ground black pepper

For the topping:
150g (5oz) ready-grated
   mozzarella or 'pizza' cheese
50g (2oz) pepperoni or ham
12 stoned black olives

Chef's Tip

You can add all kinds of toppings to pizzas – try combining tuna and onion, or ham and pineapple, or top a pizza with stir-fried vegetables (see pages 38-39).

1. To make the bread dough for the base, follow steps 1-5 on pages 74-75. When you have put it in a warm place to rise, you can start to make the tomato sauce.

Stir the sauce often, to stop it sticking.

3. Heat the sauce over a medium heat, stirring it often, for about 15 minutes or until it is really thick. Then, take the pan off the heat and leave the sauce to cool.

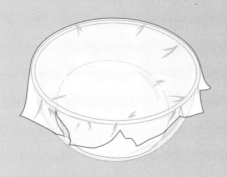

5. Put the dough back into the bowl and leave it in a warm place to rise again for about 40 minutes. Then, heat the oven to 200°C, 400°F, gas mark 6.

2. Peel and crush the garlic and put it into a saucepan with the olive oil. Then, add the chopped tomatoes, sugar, herbs and a pinch each of salt and of pepper.

4. When the dough has been in a warm place for 1½ hours, lift it out and put it on a floury surface. Knead it for about a minute, to squeeze out any air bubbles.

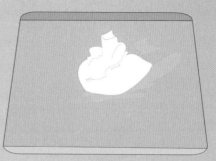

6. Using a paper towel, wipe a little oil over a large baking sheet. Then, sprinkle more flour on the floury surface and on a rolling pin. Put the dough on the surface.

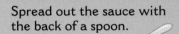
Spread out the sauce with the back of a spoon.

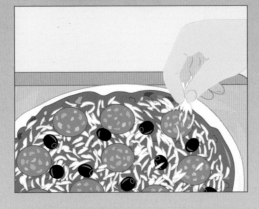

7. Roll out the dough until it is about 30cm (12in) across, then lift it onto the baking sheet. Spread the tomato sauce on it, leaving a border around the edge.

8. Sprinkle about two-thirds of the cheese over the tomato sauce. Arrange the pepperoni and olives on the cheese, then sprinkle the rest of the cheese over them.

9. Bake the pizza in the oven for about 20 minutes, until the base is crisp and the cheese is golden brown and bubbling. Then, cut it into slices with a sharp knife.

Salmon fishcakes

These crispy oven-baked fishcakes are filling and easy to make. Instead of making them with salmon, you could use haddock or smoked haddock instead.

Try serving the fishcakes with green beans. Trim off the ends of the beans and cook them in boiling water for about 10 minutes, or until they are just tender.

Ingredients:

Serves 4

350g (12oz) fresh salmon fillets
1 bay leaf
a small handful of fresh parsley
450g (1lb) potatoes
15g (½oz) butter
salt and ground black pepper
1 medium egg
about 2 tablespoons plain flour
2 slices of medium-thickness
   white bread, with the
   crusts removed
1 tablespoon sunflower oil

Keep the parsley leaves for later.

1. Put the salmon into a large pan, in a single layer. Pour in enough water to just cover it. Add the bay leaf, then break the stalks off the parsley and add them too.

The salmon turns pale pink as it cooks.

2. Heat the pan until the water boils, then reduce the heat, so that the water is just bubbling. Cook the salmon for four minutes, then take the pan off the heat.

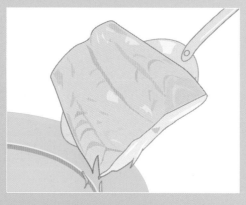

3. Using a spatula, lift out the salmon and put it onto a plate to cool. Clean the pan thoroughly, then half-fill it with cold water and add two pinches of salt.

4. Peel the potatoes and cut them into large chunks. Put them into the pan, then heat the water until it boils. Reduce the heat a little, so that the water is gently bubbling.

Squeeze fresh lemon juice over the fishcakes.

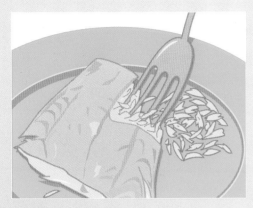

5. Cook the potatoes for 15-20 minutes, or until they are tender. While they are cooking, break the salmon into flakes, with a fork. Remove the skin and any bones.

Chef's Tip

Flaking fish is a good idea, because you should be able to see any little bones. Fillets of fish shouldn't have any bones in them, but it's a good idea to check.

Keep mashing until the potato is smooth.

6. Drain the potatoes through a colander, then tip them back into the pan. Add the butter, a pinch of salt and a pinch of black pepper, then mash the potatoes.

7. Put the parsley leaves into a mug and chop them with kitchen scissors. Then, break the egg into a bowl and beat the white and yolk with a fork.

8. Add the salmon, parsley leaves and a tablespoon of beaten egg to the potatoes and stir everything together. Then, turn on your oven to 200°C, 400°F, gas mark 6.

The flour stops the mixture sticking to your hands.

9. Divide the salmon mixture into eight pieces. Then, put a little flour on your hands. Mould each piece into a slightly flattened round, about 2cm (¾in) thick.

10. Using a food processor, make the bread into fine breadcrumbs (see page 94) and put them into a bowl. Then, using a paper towel, wipe the oil over a baking tray.

The breadcrumbs stick to the egg.

11. Brush all over a fishcake with egg, then roll the fishcake in the breadcrumbs, until it is completely covered. Then, prepare the other fishcakes in the same way.

Wear oven gloves to take the baking tray out of the oven.

12. Put the fishcakes on the baking tray and put them in the oven for 10 minutes. Lift them out and turn them, then cook them for 10 more minutes, until they are crispy.

Rice

Rice is often eaten with meat, fish or vegetables. Here, you can find out how to cook it and some information about different kinds of rice, too.

Ways to cook

Rice can be boiled or steamed. Some rice needs to be soaked before it's cooked, so always check the instructions on the packet. Also look to see how much rice you need for each person. If it doesn't say on the packet, 75g (3oz) will be about right for each person, to accompany a main meal.

White rice has had its outer coating removed.

'Easy-cook' rice is treated so that the grains don't stick together when the rice is cooked.

Boiling in lots of water

1. Half-fill a pan with water and add a pinch of salt. Heat the water until it boils, add the rice and bring it back to the boil.

2. Turn down the heat a little and cook the rice for as long as it says on the packet. Then, drain it through a large sieve.

Mixed rice contains two or more different kinds of rice. The rice grains are treated so that they will cook in the same amount of time.

Just enough water

Brown rice needs an extra half cup of water per person.

The water should be bubbling gently.

Don't lift the lid while the rice is cooking.

1. To cook rice without having to drain it, put one cup of rice and two cups of water for each person in a pan.

2. Add a pinch of salt and heat the water until it boils. Stir the rice, then reduce the heat a little. Put a lid on the pan.

3. Cook the rice for as long as it says on the packet. If any water is left, heat the pan for another minute.

Chef's Tip

When you cook rice, if the water turns thick and sticky, tip the rice into a sieve and rinse it with boiling water.

Brown rice still has its outer coating and is chewier than white rice. It needs to be cooked for longer than white rice.

Arborio rice is sticky and is used to make risotto (see pages 36-37).

Wild rice is not actually rice at all. It's a type of seed from the USA and Canada. It should be soaked for at least an hour, then cooked for about 40 minutes.

Thai or Jasmine rice is very sticky, which makes it easier to eat with chopsticks. Here you can see it cooked and uncooked.

Basmati rice needs to be soaked before it's cooked. Try eating it with creamy chicken curry (pages 42-43).

Steamed rice

Steaming works better with white rice than brown rice.

Red Carmargue rice has a nutty taste. It needs to be washed then boiled for about 30 minutes.

1. Soak the rice in cold water for one hour, then drain it through a sieve. Half-fill a pan with water and heat it until it boils.

2. Put the rice into a steamer. Put the steamer on top of the pan. Cook the rice for at least 20 minutes, until it is tender.

Short-grain or pudding rice is used to make rice pudding, which is a sweet dish.

33

Chilli con carne

The name of this spicy dish means 'chilli with meat'. It is often served with rice, but can also be spooned into a jacket potato (see page 65).

Ingredients:

Serves 4

half a beef or vegetable stock cube
1 onion
1 clove of garlic
1½ tablespoons vegetable oil
450g (1lb) minced beef
2-3 teaspoons mild chilli powder
1 teaspoon ground cumin
400g (14oz) can red kidney beans
400g (14oz) can chopped tomatoes
1 tablespoon tomato purée
1 teaspoon soft dark brown sugar
half a teaspoon of dried mixed herbs
salt and ground black pepper

1. Put the stock cube into a heatproof jug and pour in 225ml (8 fl oz) of boiling water. Stir the stock until the cube has dissolved, then put the jug to one side.

2. Peel the onion and cut it in half. Cut it into slices, then cut the slices into small pieces. Peel and crush the garlic. Put the pieces of onion, garlic and oil into a large saucepan.

3. Gently heat the pan over a low heat for 10 minutes, stirring the onion and garlic frequently. Then, increase the heat to medium and add the minced beef.

4. Cook the beef for about 10 minutes, or until it is brown all over. Break up any lumps with a wooden spoon and keep stirring it as it cooks.

Chef's Tip

You're about to add chilli powder to the mince. If you pour spices from the jar into a spoon over a pan, you may add too much, so do it away from the pan instead.

5. Take the pan off the heat and stir in the chilli powder and cumin. Then, open the can of kidney beans. Pour them into a colander and rinse them under cold water.

6. Add the beans, tomatoes, stock, tomato purée, sugar and herbs to the pan. Add two pinches of salt and of pepper, then stir everything together.

The steam escapes through the gap.

7. Put the pan back on the heat and heat it until the chilli con carne boils. Stir the chilli, then reduce the heat to low. Put a lid on the pan, leaving a small gap.

8. Cook the chilli for 15 minutes, then remove the lid and cook it for another 15 minutes. Make sure you stir the chilli every now and then, to stop it from sticking.

Vegetable risotto

Risotto is made with arborio rice, which becomes sticky when it's cooked. In this recipe, the rice is cooked in stock and vegetables are added as it cooks. If you're really hungry, serve the risotto with bread rolls.

Ingredients:

Serves 4

4 ripe tomatoes
50g (2oz) frozen peas
100g (4oz) broccoli
50g (2oz) Parmesan cheese
1 onion
1 clove of garlic
15g (½oz) butter
1 tablespoon of olive oil
200g (7oz) arborio (risotto) rice
1 vegetable stock cube
2 tablespoons chopped fresh
  parsley
salt and ground black pepper

1. Cut a cross on the bottom of each tomato with a sharp knife. Put the tomatoes in a heatproof bowl, then fill another bowl with cold water.

The skins should start to peel after about a minute or so.

2. Pour boiling water over the tomatoes. When their skins start to peel, lift them out with a slotted spoon and put them into the cold water for two minutes.

Throw away the skins, cores and seeds.

3. Lift the tomatoes out and peel off the skins. Cut each tomato into quarters, then scoop out the seeds and cut out the cores. Then, cut the quarters into small pieces.

4. Put the peas onto a plate to defrost. Cut the end off the stem of the broccoli and throw it away. Cut off the curly bits and cut them into pieces, then slice the stem.

5. Grate the Parmesan on the fine holes on a grater. Then, peel an onion and cut it in half. Finely slice it, then cut the slices into small pieces. Peel the clove of garlic.

Keep stirring the onion and garlic.

6. Put the butter, oil and onion into a large saucepan. Crush the garlic into the pan, then heat the pan over a medium heat for five minutes, or until the onion is soft.

7. Take the pan off the heat. Add the rice to the pan and stir it in, to coat the grains of rice with the butter mixture. Then, put the stock cube into another pan.

8. Add 1 litre (1¾ pints) of boiling water and stir it well. Gently heat the stock, until it is just bubbling, then add a ladleful to the rice and put the rice back on the heat.

Use a wooden spoon.

You may not need to use all the stock.

9. Gently stir the rice until nearly all of the liquid has been absorbed. Then, add the broccoli and another ladleful of stock. Each time the stock is absorbed, stir in more.

10. About 15 minutes after you added the first stock, stir in the peas. Keep adding ladlefuls of stock and stirring them in, until the rice is creamy and just tender.

11. Take the pan off the heat and cover it with a lid. Leave it for three minutes, then stir in the tomatoes, parsley, Parmesan and two pinches of salt and of pepper.

Chicken stir-fry

Stir-fries are quick and easy to cook. In this recipe, the chicken is soaked in a marinade, which is a sauce that helps to make meat tender and tasty.

Ingredients:

Serves 4

2cm (1in) piece of fresh root ginger
1 tablespoon clear honey
3 tablespoons dark soy sauce
1 tablespoon fresh lemon juice
3 skinless, boneless chicken breasts
2 carrots
1 yellow or red pepper
8 spring onions
100g (4oz) mangetout
2 tablespoons sunflower oil
half a teaspoon of cornflour
a vegetable stock cube

Chef's Tip

When you cook a stir-fry, you add lots of different ingredients and cook them quickly, so you prepare all the ingredients before you start cooking.

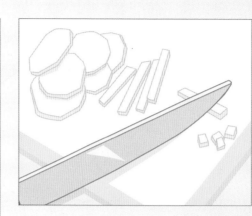

1. Cut the brown skin off the ginger and throw it away. Cut the ginger into thin slices and cut the slices into thin sticks. Then, cut the sticks into tiny pieces.

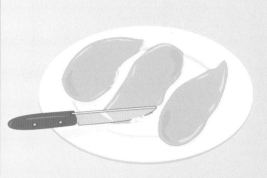

2. For the marinade, put the ginger in a bowl. Add the honey, soy sauce and lemon juice. Then, cut any bits of white fat off the chicken breasts and throw them away.

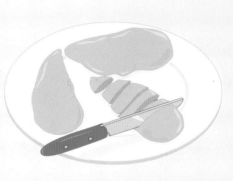

3. Cut the chicken into strips. Stir the strips into the marinade, then wash your hands (see the Chef's tip on page 42). Then, peel the carrots with a potato peeler.

You don't need the ends or the seeds.

4. Cut the ends off the pepper, remove the seeds and cut it into strips. Then, cut the ends off the carrots. Cut them in half, then in half again, then into thin sticks.

Cut the mangetout lengthways.

5. Cut the ends and outer layer off the spring onions. Cut the stalks off the mangetout. Then, cut the onions into diagonal slices and cut the mangetout in half.

6. Put the stock cube into a heatproof jug. Pour in 300ml (½ pint) of boiling water and stir it until the cube dissolves. Then, put the jug to one side.

Use a spoon to
add the chicken.

7. Heat one tablespoon of oil in a large frying pan, for one minute, over a medium heat. Carefully add the chicken to the pan, but don't add the marinade yet.

The stir-fry can be served with egg noodles or rice.

8. Cook the chicken for five minutes, stirring it all the time. Then, take it out of the pan with a slotted spoon and put it on a plate. Put the chicken to one side.

Stir the vegetables all the time.

Stir the stock with a fork, as you add the marinade.

9. Add the other tablespoon of oil to the pan and heat it for about 20 seconds. Then, add the pieces of carrot and mangetout and cook them for two minutes.

10. Add the spring onions and strips of pepper and cook them for one minute. Mix the cornflour into the marinade, then mix the marinade into the stock.

11. Pour the stock into the pan and stir everything well. Then, stir in the chicken. Heat the stir-fry until the stock boils, then gently cook everything for three minutes.

Herbs and spices

Herbs and spices are used to flavour food. They are cooked with meat, fish and vegetables, but can also be used to add flavour to sauces, salads and even sweet things.

Bay leaves are used to flavour stews and soups, like the leek and potato soup on pages 10-11. They are removed before the food is served.

Herbs

You can use fresh or dried herbs when you cook. If a recipe uses fresh herbs but you only have dried ones, use half the amount, as dried herbs taste a lot stronger.

Parsley is used in lots of recipes. It is also used to decorate food.

Preparing herbs

Dill is eaten with fish and can also be mixed into salads.

1. Wash the herbs and dry them on some paper towels. Then, cut off any thick or woody stalks and throw them away.

Basil tastes delicious with tomatoes (see pages 48-49) and can be ripped up and scattered on salads.

Dried mixed herbs are a mixture of several different herbs and are included in all kinds of dishes.

2. Put the soft parts of the herbs into a mug. To finely chop them, snip them with kitchen scissors again and again.

Fresh coriander has a very strong flavour. It is used in the tomato salsa on pages 22-23.

Chives

Mint has a fresh taste. It is often mixed with yogurt, but is also used to decorate food.

You don't need to trim chives before you chop them. Just hold several chives together and snip them into tiny pieces.

Chives have a mild onion flavour.

Oregano is used fresh or dried.

Spices

Spices come from different parts of plants, such as berries, roots, bark and seeds. They are not always hot, but many have strong and distinctive flavours.

Most of the spices used in this book are in a crushed or powdered form. Whole spices can also be crushed, using a pestle and mortar.

Coriander seeds have a delicious, light flavour when they're crushed.

Cumin seeds are used a lot in Indian cooking.

Ground coriander tastes slightly sweet.

Cinnamon sticks

Cinnamon is the bark of a tree. The sticks are used in spicy dishes and are not eaten. Ground cinnamon is used to flavour sweet dishes, such as apple crumble (see pages 80-81).

This is ground cumin. It is strong, with a warm flavour.

Turmeric has a strong, slightly bitter flavour.

Paprika is spicy and is made from the seeds of sweet peppers.

Ginger can be used fresh, as a root (see pages 38-39), or dried and ground.

Dried chillies

Chillies are very hot and spicy. They can be bought fresh, dried or as a powder.

Ground ginger

Chilli powder

Whole nutmeg seeds are grated to make a fine powder.

Creamy chicken curry

A lot of curries are very hot and spicy, but this one is mild and creamy, with a hint of spices. Serve it with boiled or steamed rice (see pages 32-33).

Ingredients:

Serves 4

4 skinless, boneless chicken breasts
2 level teaspoons cornflour
300ml (½ pint) thick plain yogurt
1 chicken stock cube
1 onion
2 tablespoons vegetable oil
2 cloves of garlic
half a teaspoon of ground turmeric
half a teaspoon of ground ginger
1 teaspoon ground cumin
2 teaspoons ground coriander
150ml (¼ pint) coconut milk
salt and ground black pepper
2 tablespoons chopped fresh coriander

Chef's Tip

Whenever you cook chicken, you need to wash your hands before handling any other food. Make sure you use a separate chopping board or plate, too.

Throw away any bits of fat.

1. Using a sharp knife, cut any bits of white fat off the chicken breasts. Cut each chicken breast into three equal-sized pieces, then wash your hands thoroughly.

2. Put the cornflour into a bowl. Add two tablespoons of yogurt and mix them in well. Then, mix in the rest of the yogurt, a little at a time.

3. Put the stock cube into a heatproof jug and pour in 75ml (3 fl oz) of boiling water. Then, stir the water until the stock cube dissolves completely.

Stir the onion as it cooks.

4. Cut the ends off the onion and peel it. Cut it in half, then into small pieces. Put the pieces into a large saucepan with the oil. Cook them over a low heat for 10 minutes.

5. Take the pan off the heat. Then, peel and crush the garlic. Add the crushed garlic to the pan, then add the ground turmeric, ginger, cumin and coriander, too.

6. Gently heat the pan for two minutes and keep stirring it. Turn the heat down very low and add the chicken. Stir in the yogurt mixture, one tablespoon at a time.

This curry is served with Basmati rice and decorated with a sprig of fresh coriander.

If you're serving rice with the curry, you'll need to start cooking it while the chicken is cooking in step 8.

The steam escapes through the gap.

Uncooked chicken will still be pink.

7. Stir the coconut milk and stock into the mixture, a little at a time. Mix in a pinch of salt and of pepper, then put a lid on the pan, leaving a small gap on one side.

8. Cook the curry over a low heat for 30 minutes, stirring it every now and then. Then, take out a piece of chicken and cut it in half. If it is white inside, it is cooked.

9. If the chicken is slightly pink inside, cook it for another 5-10 minutes. Then, stir in the fresh coriander and serve the curry straight away.

Spaghetti bolognese

This tasty meat sauce is usually served with spaghetti, but it can also be layered with a white sauce and sheets of pasta, to make lasagne (see pages 60-61).

Ingredients:

Serves 4

1 onion
1 carrot
1 stick of celery
2 tablespoons olive oil
1 clove of garlic
450g (1lb) minced beef
1 beef or vegetable stock cube
400g (14oz) can chopped
   tomatoes
1 teaspoon dried mixed herbs
1 tablespoon tomato purée
salt and ground black pepper
half a tablespoon of olive oil
400g (14oz) dried spaghetti

Chef's Tip

To see if pasta is cooked, lift out a piece with a spoon, rinse it under cold water and bite it. It should be tender but not soggy. This is known as 'al dente' in Italy.

You don't need the ends of the celery.

1. Peel the onion and cut it in half. Slice it and chop it finely. Then, peel the carrot and cut off its ends. Cut it in half, then cut it into strips. Cut the strips into small pieces.

2. Wash the celery, and cut off its ends. Cut it into small pieces. Put the onion and the olive oil into a large saucepan. Cook them over a medium heat for five minutes.

3. Peel the garlic and crush it into the pan, then add the pieces of carrot and celery. Heat everything for two minutes, stirring them all the time with a wooden spoon.

4. Add the beef to the pan and cook it for about 10 minutes, or until it is brown all over. Break up any lumps with the spoon and keep stirring it as it cooks.

5. Put the stock cube into a heatproof jug. Add 300ml (½ pint) of boiling water, and stir it until the stock cube has dissolved. Then, add the stock to the pan.

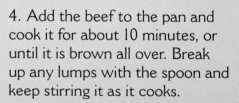

6. Add the chopped tomatoes, herbs, tomato purée and a couple of pinches of salt and of pepper to the pan. Heat the sauce until it boils, then turn down the heat.

The sauce should be gently bubbling.

Push in the ends of the spaghetti with a wooden spoon.

7. Put the lid on the pan, leaving a small gap. Cook the sauce for 40 minutes, stirring it every now and then. Then, remove the lid and cook it for 10 more minutes.

8. While the sauce is cooking, fill a large pan with water and add a large pinch of salt. Add half a tablespoon of olive oil, then heat the pan until the water boils.

9. Lower one end of the spaghetti into the water. As it softens, bend it around until it is covered by the water. Boil it for as long as it says on the packet, stirring often.

Serve the spaghetti bolognese with some grated Parmesan cheese sprinkled over the top.

10. Carefully pour the spaghetti into a colander in the sink and gently shake the colander. Then, put some spaghetti on each plate, and spoon some sauce over it.

Tagliatelle carbonara

This egg-based pasta dish is quick and simple to make. The eggs are cooked by the heat of the pasta and make a creamy sauce. Tagliatelle pasta is used here, but you can use any long thin pasta, such as spaghetti or linguine.

Ingredients:

Serves 4

1 teaspoon olive oil
150g (5oz) streaky bacon
2 cloves of garlic
1½ tablespoons olive oil
50g (2oz) Parmesan
   cheese
3 medium eggs
2 tablespoons fresh parsley,
   chopped
3 tablespoons single cream
ground black pepper
350g (12oz) dried tagliatelle

Don't crush the garlic cloves.

1. Half-fill a large saucepan with water and add a teaspoon of olive oil. Heat the water until it boils, then switch off the heat and put the pan to one side.

2. If there is rind on the bacon, cut it off with clean kitchen scissors and throw it away. Then, cut the bacon into strips and put them into a saucepan.

3. Peel the garlic and add it to the pan with 1½ tablespoons of olive oil. Heat the pan over a medium heat for 3-4 minutes, until the bacon is crispy.

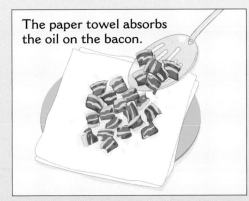

The paper towel absorbs the oil on the bacon.

4. Turn off the heat. Lift the bacon out of the pan with a spoon and put it on some paper towels. Throw away the garlic cloves, which will have added flavour.

5. Grate the cheese on the fine holes on a grater. Then, break the eggs into a bowl and add half of the cheese, the chopped parsley, the cream and a pinch of black pepper.

6. Mix everything in the bowl with a fork. Then, heat the pan of water until it is boiling again. Add the tagliatelle and cook it for as long as it says on the packet.

Chef's Tip

When you're boiling pasta, keep an eye on it, in case it boils too hard. If it looks as if it's about to boil over, turn down the heat a little, but keep the water bubbling.

7. When the pasta is cooked, turn off the heat, then pour it into a colander in the sink. Shake the colander, then tip the pasta back into the pan and add the bacon.

8. Add the egg mixture and stir it in well, until there is no liquid egg left. Then, spoon the tagliatelle into four bowls and sprinkle the rest of the cheese over the top.

Pasta with fresh tomato sauce

This pasta dish tastes really fresh and is ideal as a light meal. To make it taste really good, use the ripest tomatoes and the freshest basil you can find.

Ingredients:

Serves 4

For the sauce:
680g (1½lb) ripe tomatoes
2 cloves of garlic
1 tablespoon olive oil
a pinch of caster sugar
half a teaspoon of dried oregano
   or mixed herbs
salt and ground black pepper
about 12 fresh basil leaves

For the pasta:
1 tablespoon olive oil
salt
350g (12oz) dried pasta shapes

If you want to serve the pasta at the table, put all the pasta into a big bowl, like this, and spoon the sauce on top.

1. Cut a cross on the bottom of each tomato with a sharp knife. Put the tomatoes into a heatproof bowl, then fill a second bowl with cold water.

2. Pour boiling water over the tomatoes, until they are completely covered. Leave them in the water for about a minute, until their skins start to peel off.

Make sure your hands are clean.

3. Lift the tomatoes out with a slotted spoon, then put them into the cold water for two minutes. Lift them out, peel off their skins, then cut each one into quarters.

4. Scoop out the seeds with a teaspoon. Carefully cut out the green core and cut all the quarters into small pieces. Then, peel the garlic and crush it.

The steam escapes through the gap.

5. Put the garlic, a tablespoon of olive oil, the tomatoes, sugar, herbs and a pinch of salt and of pepper into a saucepan. Heat the pan over a medium heat for two minutes.

6. Cover the pan with a lid, leaving a small gap, and turn down the heat. Cook the sauce over a low heat for about 15 minutes, stirring it often, to stop it sticking.

7. Meanwhile, half-fill a large pan with water. Add a tablespoon of olive oil and a pinch of salt. Heat the water until it boils, then add the pasta to the pan and stir it.

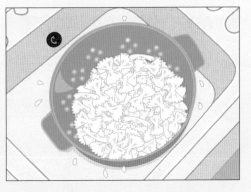

8. Heat the pan until the water is boiling again. Then, turn down the heat, so that the water is bubbling more gently. Cook the pasta for as long as it says on the packet.

9. While the pasta is cooking, stir the tomato sauce every now and then. Pour the cooked pasta into a colander and drain it well, by gently shaking the colander.

10. Rip the basil leaves into small pieces and stir them into the tomato sauce. Then, spoon the pasta into four bowls and spoon the tomato sauce over the top.

This kind of pasta is farfalle, but you can use any shape.

49

Macaroni cheese

This macaroni cheese has a crunchy cheese topping. It's quick to cook and goes really well with a sliced tomato salad.

Ingredients:

Serves 4

salt
225g (8oz) dried macaroni
225g (8oz) Cheddar cheese
small amount of butter
50g (2oz) butter or margarine
50g (2oz) plain flour
750ml (1¼ pints) milk
half a teaspoon of mustard
ground black pepper
2 slices of bread, crusts removed

For the tomato salad:
8 ripe tomatoes
25g (1oz) chopped chives

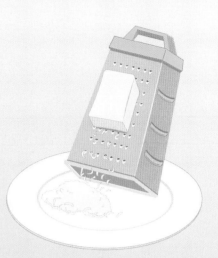

1. Half-fill a saucepan with water and add two pinches of salt. Heat the water until it boils, then add the macaroni. Cook the macaroni for as long as it says on the packet.

2. Meanwhile, grate the cheese on the medium holes on a grater. When the macaroni is cooked, pour it into a colander and drain it well, by gently shaking the colander.

Don't put the pan back on the heat.

Add the flour slowly, to avoid making lumps.

3. Spoon the macaroni back into the pan and stir in a little butter, to stop the pieces sticking together. Then, cover the pan with a lid, to keep the macaroni warm.

4. Put 50g (2oz) butter into a large pan, and heat it over a low heat until it melts. Take the pan off the heat, then stir in the flour, a little at a time.

Use a wooden spoon.

It's really important to keep stirring the sauce.

Chef's Tip

5. Add a little milk to the pan. Stir it in really well, until the mixture is smooth. Then, stir in a little more milk. Carry on until you have added all the milk.

6. Heat the sauce over a medium heat, stirring all the time, until it becomes thicker and then boils. Boil it for one minute, still stirring it, then take it off the heat.

If your sauce is a little lumpy when you take it off the heat, it's easy to make it smooth. Twist a whisk around and around in the pan, until the lumps have gone.

Keep some of the cheese for the topping.

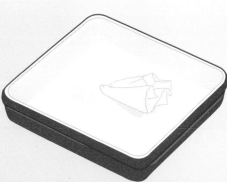

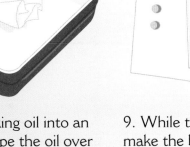

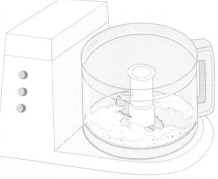

7. Stir the mustard, macaroni and a pinch of pepper into the sauce. Heat the pan for about 30 seconds, then take it off the heat. Then, stir in three-quarters of the cheese.

8. Pour a little cooking oil into an ovenproof dish. Wipe the oil over the inside of the dish with a paper towel, then heat the grill to a medium heat for five minutes.

9. While the grill is heating up, make the breadcrumbs for the topping. Put the bread into a food processor (see page 94) and make it into breadcrumbs.

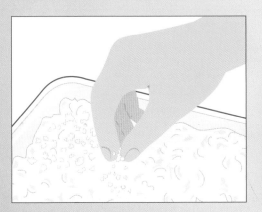

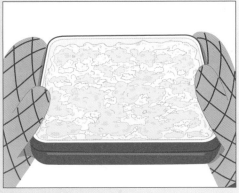

Lay the halves flat side down.

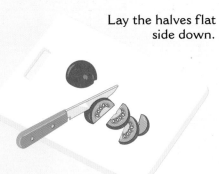

10. Spoon the macaroni into the dish and sprinkle the breadcrumbs over the top. Then, sprinkle the rest of the grated cheese over the breadcrumbs.

11. Carefully put the dish under the grill and leave the macaroni to cook for 5-6 minutes, until it turns golden. Then, carefully remove the dish, wearing oven gloves.

12. For the salad, cut the tomatoes in half, cut out the core and throw it away. Cut the tomatoes into slices, then put them into a bowl. Sprinkle chopped chives over the top.

Vegetables

Lots of the recipes in this book include vegetables, cooked in a variety of ways. On these pages, you'll find out a bit more about preparing different kinds of vegetables.

A good rinse

Unless told otherwise, always rinse vegetables and salad ingredients. However, mushrooms shouldn't be rinsed – they just need a wipe with a damp paper towel.

Hot or cold water?

Some vegetables are put in boiling water to be cooked, and others are placed in a pan of cold water and brought to the boil. In general, root vegetables (such as potatoes, carrots and parsnips) are cooked from cold, and the others are placed in water which has already boiled. To find out more about how to cook potatoes, see pages 64-65.

Find out how to prepare tomatoes in step 2 on page 4.

Chopping an onion

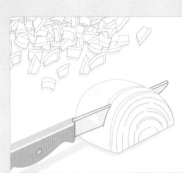

Throw the skin and ends away.

1. Using a sharp knife, carefully cut off both ends of the onion. Then, cut down one side and peel off the skin.

2. With a flat side facing down, cut the onion in half. Cut each half into slices, then chop the slices into small pieces.

Peeling garlic

Throw the ends and skin away.

1. To remove a clove from a head of garlic, press against the side of the stem. When the skin splits, break it open.

2. To peel the clove, cut off its ends, then make a cut down the skin. Then, peel off the skin with your fingers.

Preparing peppers

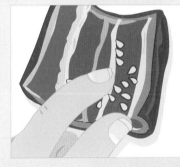

1. Using a sharp knife, carefully cut off the ends of the pepper. Then, cut the pepper in half, from top to bottom.

2. Remove the lines of white seeds with your fingers. Throw away the ends of the pepper and the seeds.

Broccoli

Floret

Throw this bit away.

1. Put the broccoli on a chopping board, and cut off the tough end of the main stem. Then, cut off the individual florets.

2. Put the florets into a colander. Rinse them thoroughly under cold running water, then shake them dry.

Mushrooms

Throw this bit away.

Wipe each mushroom with a damp paper towel, to remove any dirt. Then, cut off the end of the stem.

Cleaning leeks

Throw the ends away.

1. If a leek is dirty, cut off the tough green top and trim off the root. Then, cut all the way down, from end to end.

2. To remove any mud or dirt inside, rinse each half of the leek really well under running water, until it is clean.

3. Shake the pieces of leek to remove the water. Then, lay them on a chopping board and slice across them.

Ratatouille with butter bean mash

Ratatouille is a mixture of fresh vegetables in a tomato sauce. Here it is served with butter bean mash, making a complete vegetarian meal.

Ingredients:

Serves 4

2 onions
450g (1lb) ripe tomatoes
3 courgettes
1 aubergine, weighing about
 350g (12oz)
1 yellow or red pepper
3 tablespoons olive oil
1 clove of garlic
1 tablespoon tomato purée
half a teaspoon of dried
 oregano or mixed herbs
salt and ground black pepper
8 large basil leaves

For the butter bean mash:
two 400g (14oz) cans of
 butter beans
15g (½oz) butter
salt and ground black pepper
2 tablespoons chopped fresh
 parsley

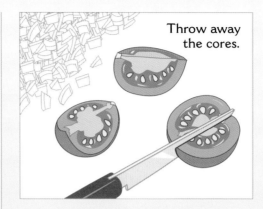

Throw away the cores.

1. Peel the onions and cut them in half. Cut them into slices, then cut the slices into small pieces. Then, peel the tomatoes, cut them into quarters and cut out the cores.

2. Cut the ends off the courgettes and throw them away. Cut each courgette in half lengthways, then cut the halves in half, to make strips. Cut the strips into chunks.

Ratatouille is also delicious served with grilled meat or fish.

3. Prepare the aubergine in the same way as the courgettes. Then, cut the ends off the yellow pepper and remove the seeds. Cut the pepper into thin strips, lengthways.

4. Put the oil and the onions into a large saucepan. Cook the onions over a low heat for about 10 minutes, until they are soft and starting to turn golden.

5. Peel and crush the garlic and add it to the pan. Then, add all of the prepared vegetables, tomato purée, herbs and a pinch of salt and of pepper. Stir everything well.

6. Cook the ratatouille over a medium heat for about three minutes, stirring it often. Then, turn down the heat, so that it is bubbling gently.

Watch out for the hot steam when you lift the lid.

7. Cover the pan with its lid and cook the ratatouille for 20 minutes, stirring it every now and then. Then, remove the lid and cook it for another 10 minutes.

You don't need the liquid from this can.

8. Meanwhile, open both cans of butter beans. Pour the contents of one can, including the liquid, into a saucepan. Pour the contents of the other can into a colander.

9. Rinse the beans in the colander with cold water, then drain them. Pour the rinsed beans into the saucepan, then add the butter and a pinch of salt and of pepper.

10. Heat the pan until the liquid is gently boiling, then turn the heat down low. Cook the beans for five minutes, until they are very soft. Then, turn off the heat.

If the mash is a little dry, mix in a few drops of milk.

11. Mash the beans well, then stir in the chopped parsley. Tear the basil leaves into small pieces and stir them into the ratatouille, before serving it with the mash.

Vegetable crumble

This savoury crumble is topped with a delicious mixture of oats, nuts and cheese. The vegetable filling includes sweet potatoes, which have a rich, sweet flavour.

Ingredients:

Serves 4

For the crumble topping:
100g (4oz) plain flour
50g (2oz) butter
50g (2oz) Cheddar cheese
25g (1oz) chopped mixed nuts
2 tablespoons rolled oats

For the vegetable filling:
2 leeks
100g (4oz) button mushrooms
1 carrot
450g (1lb) sweet potatoes
a vegetable stock cube
25g (1oz) butter
1 tablespoon plain flour
50g (2oz) cream cheese
  or mascarpone cheese
salt and ground black pepper

1. For the topping, sift the flour through a sieve into a large bowl. Cut the butter into cubes and add them to the flour. Rub the butter into the flour with your fingers.

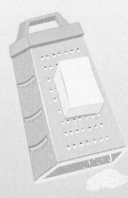

2. Grate the Cheddar cheese on the big holes on a grater. Add it to the bowl, then add the nuts and oats. Stir all the ingredients until they are mixed together well.

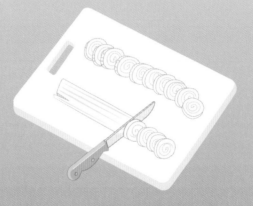

3. Heat the oven to 190°C, 375°F, gas mark 5. While it is heating up, cut the ends off the leeks. Wash the leeks thoroughly in cold water, then cut them into thin slices.

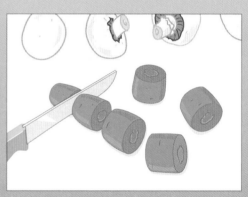

4. Wipe the mushrooms with a damp paper towel and cut off the ends. Then, peel the carrot with a potato peeler. Cut off the ends, then cut it into about six chunks.

Keep the heat low.

5. Peel the sweet potatoes. Cut each potato in half, then into 2cm (¾in) cubes. Then, put the stock cube into a heatproof jug and add 150ml (¼ pint) of boiling water.

6. Stir the water until the stock cube has completely dissolved. Then, put the butter into a large pan and gently heat the pan over a low heat, until the butter melts.

7. Put the leeks into the pan and put on the lid, leaving a gap. Cook the leeks for three minutes. Gently shake the pan every now and then, to stop them from sticking.

Chef's Tip

8. Remove the lid, then add the mushrooms, carrots and sweet potatoes to the pan. Cook them gently for five minutes, stirring them often.

In the next step, you're going to add the flour and stock to the pan. To stop the flour going lumpy, add a little stock at a time, mix it in, then add some more.

9. Sprinkle the flour over the vegetables and stir it in well. Pour in the stock. Then, stir in the cream cheese and add two pinches of salt and of pepper.

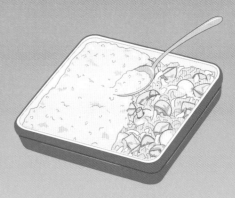

10. Heat the vegetable mixture over a medium heat for two minutes, so that it is bubbling gently. Then, spoon the mixture into an ovenproof dish.

11. Spoon the topping over the vegetables. Then, put the dish on a baking tray. Bake the crumble in the oven for 30-35 minutes or until the topping is golden brown.

Lamb kebabs

As in the stir-fry on pages 38-39, the meat in this recipe is soaked in a marinade. The kebabs are delicious in a pitta bread with shredded lettuce, cucumber, mint and lemon juice.

Ingredients:

Serves 4

For the marinade:
1 tablespoon of fresh lemon juice
4 tablespoons olive oil
a large pinch of dried oregano
salt and ground black pepper
1 clove of garlic

For the kebabs:
2 large lamb steaks, each about
   175g (6oz)
1 red onion
1 red pepper
2 courgettes

8 kebab or satay sticks

Chef's Tip

To avoid burning the kebabs, don't put them too close to the grill. When they are on the rack, they should be about 8cm (3in) below the grill.

1. For the marinade, put the lemon juice into a bowl with the oil, dried oregano and a pinch of salt and of pepper. Peel the garlic, crush it into the bowl and stir everything well.

Throw away the bone and fat.

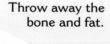

3. Using a sharp knife, carefully cut out any bone and trim the fat off the lamb. Then, cut the lamb into 2cm (¾in) cubes. Add them to the marinade and stir them in well.

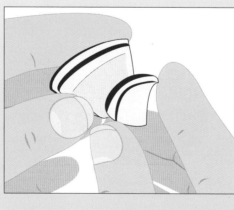

5. Cut the ends off the onion and peel it. Cut the onion in half, then in half again. Then, cut across each quarter. Separate each chunk into double slices, like this.

2. If you're using wooden sticks, put them into a dish of water to soak. This helps to stop them from burning when you put them under the grill.

4. Cover the bowl with plastic foodwrap. Put it in a fridge for at least an hour, so that the meat soaks in the marinade. While it is soaking, prepare the vegetables.

Throw away the ends and the seeds.

6. Cut the ends off the red pepper. Remove the seeds. Cut the pepper into 2cm (¾in) squares. Then, cut off the ends of the courgettes and cut them into thick slices.

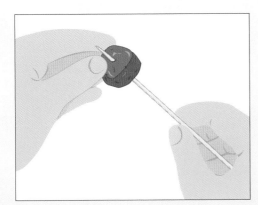

7. Take the wooden sticks out of the water. Then, carefully push one cube of lamb onto each wooden stick, being careful of the pointed end.

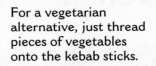

For a vegetarian alternative, just thread pieces of vegetables onto the kebab sticks.

Carefully take the pieces of lamb and vegetables off the kebab sticks before serving them.

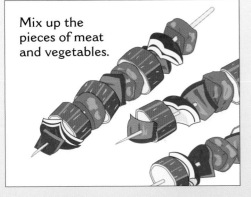

Mix up the pieces of meat and vegetables.

8. Push pieces of vegetables and lamb onto the wooden sticks, until you have used up all of the pieces. Then, heat the grill, to a medium temperature, for five minutes.

Lay the kebabs on the rack in a grill pan.

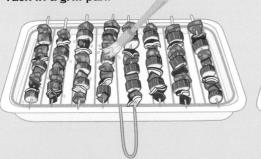

9. Brush the vegetables with the marinade, so that they don't dry out while they're cooking. Then, put the kebabs under the grill and cook them for 10 minutes.

10. After 10 minutes, carefully turn the kebabs over. Spoon the rest of the marinade over them, then grill them for another 5-10 minutes, or until they are browned.

Squeeze fresh lemon juice over the cooked lamb.

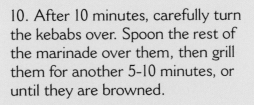

Lasagne

Lasagne is made up of layers of white sauce, bolognese sauce and pasta. For a vegetarian alternative, use ratatouille (see pages 54-55) instead of bolognese sauce.

Ingredients:

Serves 4

For the bolognese sauce:
1 onion
1 carrot
1 stick of celery
2 tablespoons olive oil
1 clove of garlic
450g (1lb) lean minced beef
1 beef or vegetable stock cube
400g (14oz) can chopped
   tomatoes
1 tablespoon tomato purée
1 teaspoon dried mixed herbs
salt and ground black pepper

For the white sauce:
15g (½oz) butter
15g (½oz) plain flour
300ml (½ pint) milk
a pinch of grated nutmeg
salt and ground black pepper

175g (6oz) easy-cook dried
   lasagne
25g (1oz) Parmesan cheese

Remember to keep stirring the bolognese sauce.

1. To make the bolognese sauce, follow steps 1-7 on pages 44-45. When you get to step 7, and the bolognese sauce is gently bubbling, start to make the white sauce.

2. To make the white sauce, follow steps 4-6 on pages 50-51, using the amounts in this recipe. Take the pan off the heat, then stir in a pinch of salt, of pepper and of nutmeg.

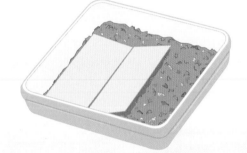

3. Heat the oven to 180°C, 350°F, gas mark 4. While it is heating up, wipe a paper towel in some butter, then wipe butter over the inside of an ovenproof dish.

4. Spoon half of the bolognese sauce into the dish and spread it out with the back of the spoon. Then, place a single layer of lasagne on top of the sauce.

Chef's Tip

If the sheets of lasagne don't fit the shape of your dish, break some of them into smaller pieces. Lay down the big pieces first, then fill in the gaps with small pieces.

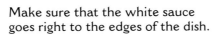

Make sure that the white sauce goes right to the edges of the dish.

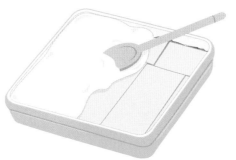

5. Spoon the rest of the bolognese sauce over the lasagne, then add another layer of lasagne. Then, spoon the white sauce over the top, so that the lasagne is covered.

6. Grate the Parmesan cheese on the fine holes on a grater, then sprinkle it over the top. Then, put the dish on a baking sheet, in case any sauce bubbles over.

7. Bake the lasagne in the oven for 35-45 minutes, or until the top is browned and bubbling. Then, carefully lift it out, wearing oven gloves. It will be very hot.

8. Push a sharp knife into the middle of the lasagne. If it is cooked, the knife will slide in easily. If it's not cooked, cook it for another 5-10 minutes.

Let the lasagne cool for five minutes, then serve it with a crunchy green salad (see pages 8-9).

Oven-roasted vegetables

This recipe is a really easy way to cook potatoes and other vegetables in the same tin. You can serve them with meat or fish or on their own with grated cheese.

Ingredients:

Serves 4

450g (1lb) small equal-sized
   new potatoes
2 carrots
2 courgettes
2 red onions
2½ tablespoons sunflower,
   vegetable or olive oil
salt and ground black pepper

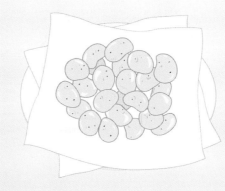

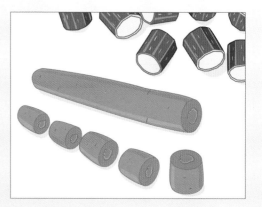

1. Put a large roasting tin into the oven. Then, heat the oven to 200°C, 400°F, gas mark 6. Scrub the potatoes clean, then dry them on some paper towels.

2. Peel the carrots with a potato peeler and cut off the ends. Cut the ends off the courgettes, too. Then, cut each courgette and carrot into about five pieces.

Spoon the vegetables into a dish, if you're serving them at the table.

Cut through the root.

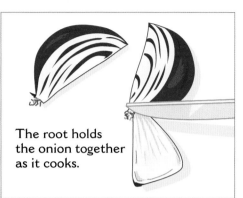

The root holds the onion together as it cooks.

3. Cut the top off the onions. Peel the skin down as far as the root at the bottom, and pull it off. Then, cut each onion into six wedges, from top to bottom.

4. Peel the outer layer of onion off each wedge, as far as the root, and carefully cut it off with a sharp knife. Then, pull any hairy bits off the roots.

5. Put the potatoes into a plastic food bag, then add a tablespoon of olive oil. Hold the bag tightly and shake it, to coat the potatoes all over with oil.

Wear oven gloves – the tin will be very hot.

Turning the vegetables helps them to brown evenly as they cook.

6. Tip the potatoes into a bowl. Put the onion wedges and carrots into the bag and add another tablespoon of oil. Shake the bag, to coat the vegetables.

7. Add the onions and carrots to the bowl. Then, take the hot tin out of the oven and tip the vegetables into it. Spread them out in a single layer.

8. Put the vegetables in the oven and cook them for 15 minutes. Then, wearing oven gloves, carefully lift them out of the oven, and turn them with a spatula.

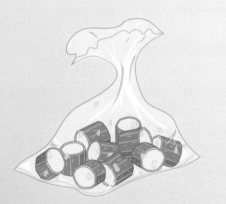

9. While the vegetables are in the oven, put the pieces of courgette in the bag with half a tablespoon of oil. Shake the bag, to cover the courgette pieces with oil.

10. Add the courgette pieces to the tin and sprinkle all the vegetables with a pinch of salt and of pepper. Then, put them back in the oven for 10 minutes.

11. Take the vegetables out of the oven and turn them again. Then, put them back in the oven for another 10 minutes, or until they are slightly browned.

Potatoes

Potatoes can be cooked in lots of different ways. On these pages you can find out about different kinds of potatoes, and some of the ways in which you can cook them.

New and not so new

There are two main types of potato – 'new' potatoes and 'old' ones. New potatoes are small, and don't need to be peeled. 'Old' potatoes have grown for longer and are bigger. Their skins are usually peeled off before they're cooked.

Are they cooked?

Potatoes need to be cooked until they're soft, but different kinds cook at different speeds. To check that they're cooked, push the point of a sharp knife into a potato. If the point goes in easily, it's cooked. If the potato is still a little hard, cook them for a little longer.

New potatoes are not always smooth and round. These thin, knobbly ones are Anya potatoes.

Some new potatoes look clean, but others are really muddy. They need to be gently scrubbed clean.

Peeling and boiling potatoes

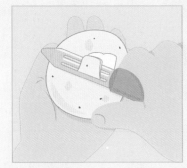

1. Rinse the potatoes. To peel each one, hold it in your hand and scrape it with a peeler again and again to remove the skin.

2. If there are spots ('eyes') on the potatoes, cut them out with a sharp knife. Then, cut the potatoes into chunks.

Add a pinch of salt.

3. Put the potatoes into a pan of cold water. Heat the water until it boils. Reduce the heat so that the water is boiling gently.

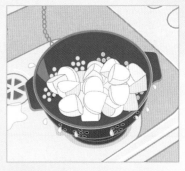

4. Put on the lid, leaving a small gap, and cook the potatoes for 20 minutes. Then, carefully drain them through a colander.

These long, thin potatoes are sweet potatoes.

The potatoes above are 'old' potatoes. They are good for baking in their 'jackets' or skins.

New potatoes

Use a clean brush.

1. Gently scrub the potatoes. Then, half-fill a pan with water and add a pinch of salt. Heat the water until it boils.

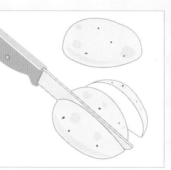

Add the potatoes with a spoon.

2. Put the potatoes into the pan. Bring them to the boil, then reduce the heat. Boil them for 15-20 minutes, then drain them.

Jacket potatoes

1. Heat your oven to 180°C, 350°F, gas mark 4. Scrub some big 'old' potatoes with a brush, to remove any dirt.

Use a fork to prick the potato several times.

2. Prick the skins, then bake the potatoes on a baking tray in the oven for 1¼-1½ hours. Check that they are cooked.

Mashing

The mash should be smooth and creamy.

Boil some 'old' potatoes, drain them and put them back into the pan, with a little butter, pepper and milk. Mash the potatoes.

Potato wedges

1. Heat the oven to 200°C, 400°F, gas mark 6. Scrub some 'old' potatoes clean. Cut them in half, then into chunky wedges.

2. Spoon a tablespoon of oil onto a baking tray and add the wedges. Mix them with your hands to lightly coat them with oil.

Cook the wedges until they are golden brown.

3. Cook the wedges in the oven for 40-45 minutes. Carefully lift them out and turn them every 15 minutes.

Fish pie

This pie is a delicious combination of haddock, prawns and spring onions, topped with a layer of golden mashed potato. It is best to make it in a fairly deep ovenproof dish.

Ingredients:

Serves 4

half a fish or vegetable
   stock cube
450g (1lb) haddock
450ml (¾ pint) milk
1 bay leaf
salt and ground black pepper
900g (2lb) potatoes
100g (4oz) butter, preferably
   unsalted
6 spring onions
50g (2oz) plain white flour
100g (4oz) cooked peeled
   prawns, defrosted if frozen
2 tablespoons chopped fresh
   parsley
1 tablespoon fresh lemon juice

1. Put the stock cube into a heatproof jug. Then, pour in 150ml (¼ pint) of boiling water and stir it until the stock cube has completely dissolved.

2. Put the fish into a pan and pour in the milk and stock. Add the bay leaf and a pinch of salt and of pepper. Heat the mixture over a medium heat, until it is just boiling.

The milk mixture will be used to make the sauce.

Cook the potatoes while the milk is cooling.

3. Reduce the heat to low and heat the mixture for five minutes. Then, turn off the heat and lift the fish onto a plate. Carefully pour the milk mixture into a jug to cool.

4. Peel the potatoes, cut them into small cubes and put them into the pan. Cover them with cold water and add a pinch of salt. When the milk is cool, remove the bay leaf.

5. Heat the water until it boils, then reduce the heat, so that it is bubbling gently. Put a lid on the pan and cook the potatoes for 15 minutes, or until they are soft.

6. While the potatoes are cooking, break the fish into flakes with a fork. Then, drain the potatoes through a colander and tip them back into the pan.

7. Add half of the butter and a pinch of pepper to the potatoes, then mash them until they are smooth. Then, put the rest of the butter into another saucepan.

Use a low heat.

Stir the mixture as it cooks.

Stir the sauce all the time.

8. Cut the ends off the spring onions. Remove the outer layer and slice the onions thinly. Then, melt the butter, add the onion slices and cook them for two minutes.

9. Add a spoonful of flour and stir it in. Stir in the rest of the flour, a spoonful at a time. Cook the mixture for one minute, then take the pan off the heat.

10. Add a little fishy milk mixture from the jug and stir it in. Then, stir in the rest of the milk, a little at a time. Heat the sauce over a medium heat, until it boils.

Spoon the fish pie onto four plates and garnish each serving with a sprig of parsley.

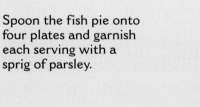

Lift out the pie when the top has turned golden.

11. Boil the sauce for one minute, still stirring it, then add the fish, prawns, parsley and lemon juice. Heat the mixture for three more minutes, then take it off the heat.

12. Heat the grill to a medium heat for five minutes. Spoon the mixture into an ovenproof dish and spoon the potato over the top. Cook the pie under the grill for five minutes.

Herby roast chicken

In this recipe, lemon and herb butter is pushed under the chicken's skin. The butter melts and adds lemon and herb flavours to the chicken. It also helps to make the meat tender.

Ingredients:

Serves 4

50g (2oz) butter, at room temperature
3 sprigs of fresh parsley, chopped
1 lemon
salt and ground black pepper
1 onion
1 roasting chicken, about 1½kg (3½lb), defrosted if frozen
1 bay leaf
1 tablespoon sunflower oil

1. Heat the oven to 190°C, 375°F, gas mark 5. Put the butter into a small bowl and stir it hard with a wooden spoon, to soften it. Then, add the chopped parsley.

2. Grate the rind of the lemon on the fine holes on a grater, until you have about half a teaspoonful. Add the rind to the butter, then cut the lemon into quarters.

You can cook the chicken with oven-roasted vegetables (see pages 62-63), but you'll need to cook the vegetables for 5-10 minutes longer than it says in the recipe.

Remove any
lemon pips.

3. Squeeze the juice from one lemon quarter into the bowl. Add a large pinch of salt and pepper and mix well. Peel an onion, cut it in half and put it to one side.

Dry inside the
chicken's
body, too.

4. Line a roasting tin with kitchen foil. Then, take the string off the chicken's legs. Wash the chicken and put it into the tin. Pat the chicken dry with a paper towel.

5. Cut out the large piece of fat from inside the chicken. Then, push the onion, the remaining three pieces of lemon and the bay leaf into the cavity in the chicken.

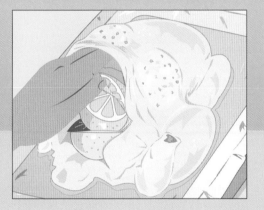

6. Gently push your fingers under the skin over the breast meat, to make a pocket on each side. Then, push the herby butter into the pockets and smooth down the skin.

7. Rub the oil all over the chicken, then wash your hands well. Put the chicken into the oven. After 45 minutes, lift it out carefully, wearing oven gloves.

Use a large metal spoon.

8. Very carefully, tilt the tin, so that the juices run into one end. Then, scoop them up and spoon them over the chicken. This helps to keep the meat moist as it cooks.

9. Put the chicken back into the oven and cook it for another 45 minutes. Check it every so often and if it starts to look dry, lift it out and spoon juices over it again.

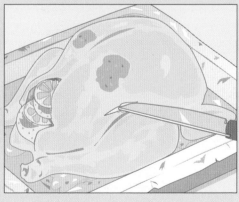

10. Push the point of a sharp knife into the meat beside a leg. If the meat looks pink, the chicken is not cooked enough, so cook it for another 10 minutes.

The juices sink back into
the meat and make it easier
to cut up the chicken.

11. Push a large wooden spoon into the cavity and carefully lift the chicken onto a warm plate. Leave the chicken for 10 minutes, before cutting it into pieces.

Oven-baked salmon

In this recipe, fillets of salmon are baked in parcels made from foil, with thin strips of carrot and leek. Lemon butter adds a fresh flavour and keeps the fish tender.

Ingredients:

Serves 4

a leek
1 carrot
50g (2oz) butter, at room
    temperature
1 lemon
salt and ground black pepper
4 salmon fillets, each about
    150g (5oz)

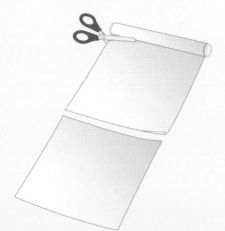

1. Heat the oven to 200°C, 400°F, gas mark 6. While it is heating up, cut four 30cm (12in) squares of kitchen foil and put them to one side for later.

Serve the salmon with boiled new potatoes or mashed potato (see pages 64-65).

You only need half of the leek.

2. Cut the leek in half. Cut off the white root and throw it away. Then, cut across one half, to make it into two chunks. Cut the chunks into lots of thin strips.

3. Peel the carrot with a potato peeler, then cut off the ends. Cut the carrot into two or three chunks, then cut them in half, lengthways. Cut the halves into thin strips.

Use the fine holes on the grater.

You'll use the rest of the juice later on.

4. Put half of the butter into a small bowl and stir it hard with a wooden spoon, until it is soft. Then, grate the rind of the lemon, until you have half a teaspoonful.

5. Cut the lemon in half. Squeeze it on a lemon squeezer, then add a teaspoon of juice, the grated rind and a pinch of salt and of pepper to the butter. Mix everything well.

6. Run your fingers all over each salmon fillet, to feel for any bones which are sticking out. If you find any, pull them out and throw them away.

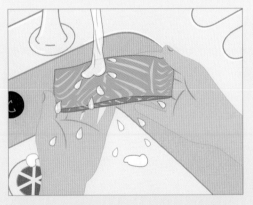

Don't use the lemon butter.

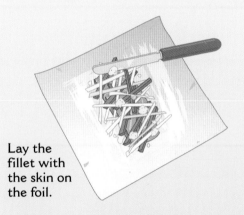

Lay the fillet with the skin on the foil.

7. Using a sharp knife, trim off any fat from the fillets and throw it away. Rinse them under cold water to remove any loose scales, then put the fillets on a clean plate.

8. Using a paper towel, rub the remaining butter over the foil squares, stopping 5cm (2in) away from the edges. Pat the fillets dry with more paper towels.

9. Place one fillet on each square. Sprinkle a teaspoon of lemon juice and strips of carrot and leek over each one. Then, put small pieces of the lemon butter over the top.

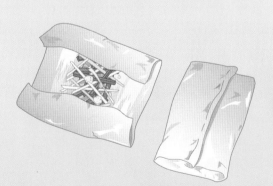

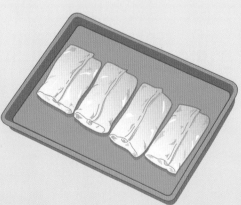

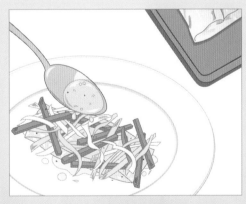

10. To make the parcels, fold the top and bottom of each foil square over the fillet. Then, pull the sides together and squeeze the foil, to seal the parcels.

11. Put the parcels onto a baking tray, then bake them in the oven for 15-20 minutes. Then, lift them out and let them cool on the baking tray for five minutes.

12. Open the foil parcels very carefully, watching out for the hot steam inside. Lift the fillets out with a fish slice, then spoon the vegetables and juices over them.

One-pot chicken casserole

This Mediterranean-style chicken casserole is a whole meal in one. There is no need to cook extra potatoes or vegetables, as they're already in the casserole.

Ingredients:

Serves 4

450g (1lb) potatoes
1 chicken or vegetable stock cube
1 yellow or red pepper
1 onion
4 skinless, boneless chicken breasts
2 tablespoons vegetable oil
1 clove of garlic
2 teaspoons plain flour
400g (14oz) can chopped tomatoes
1 teaspoon dried mixed herbs
ground black pepper
12 stoned black olives

a large oven-proof casserole dish

Slice each half before you cut it into chunks.

1. Peel the potatoes and cut them in half. Cut each half into 3cm (1in) cubes. Then, put the cubes into a saucepan and pour in cold water until they are covered.

Leave a gap, so that the steam can escape.

2. Heat the water until it boils, then reduce the heat slightly, so that it is bubbling. Put the lid on the pan and cook the potatoes for five minutes, then drain them.

You'll find it easier to serve the casserole if you use a ladle, as there is a lot of sauce.

3. Put the stock cube into a heatproof jug. Pour in 225ml (8 fl oz) of boiling water and stir it until the stock cube has dissolved. Put the potatoes and stock to one side.

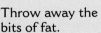
Throw away the bits of fat.

Cook the chicken until it is lightly browned.

4. Cut the ends off the pepper and remove the seeds. Cut the pepper into thick slices. Then, cut off the ends of the onion and peel it. Cut it in half, slice it and chop it finely.

5. Cut any bits of white fat off the chicken breasts and cut each one into three or four pieces. Wash your hands well. Then, heat the oven to 160°C, 325°F, gas mark 3.

6. Put one tablespoon of oil into a large non-stick frying pan and heat it over a medium heat for about 30 seconds. Carefully add the chicken and cook it for about 5-6 minutes.

7. Spoon the chicken into a casserole dish. Put the onion and the remaining oil into the frying pan. Peel and crush the garlic and add it, then cook them for 7-8 minutes.

8. Take the pan off the heat, then sprinkle the flour over the top of the onion mixture. Stir it in well, then add a little stock. Stir well, then add some more stock.

9. Stir in the rest of the stock, a little at a time, then put the frying pan back on the heat. Heat it until the stock boils, stirring all the time. Then, take it off the heat.

10. Spoon everything in the pan, including any liquid, into the casserole dish. Then, add the chopped tomatoes, herbs and two pinches of pepper.

11. Add the yellow pepper and the potatoes, then stir everything well. Put the lid on the casserole, then put it in the oven for 1¼ hours. Drain the olives through a sieve.

12. After 1¼ hours, take the casserole dish out of the oven and stir in the olives. Then, cook the casserole for another 10 minutes, or until everything is cooked.

Bread

These pages show you how to make bread dough into rolls, but the same recipe can be used to make a pizza base (see pages 28-29). You need to give yourself plenty of time to make the dough, because you need to leave it to rise.

Flour power

Bread is made with special flour called 'strong flour' or 'bread flour' and yeast. Gentle heat makes the yeast rise, which makes the dough grow. To make the yeast rise, you'll need to leave the dough in a warm place, like an airing cupboard or a warm kitchen.

Bread rolls

Ingredients:

Makes 12 rolls

450g (1lb) strong white
　　bread flour
a teaspoon of salt
2 teaspoons dried
　　easy-blend yeast
300ml (½ pint) warm
　　water, which has
　　been boiled
2 tablespoons olive or
　　vegetable oil

1. Sift the flour and the salt into a large mixing bowl, through a sieve. Then, add the yeast and stir it in.

2. Make a hollow in the middle of the flour. Pour the warm water into a jug and add the oil, then pour them into the hollow.

3. Stir everything with a wooden spoon, to make a soft dough. Then, dust a clean work surface with flour.

To make a floury bread roll, brush the uncooked roll with milk, then sift plain flour over it, through a sieve.

4. Put the dough on the work surface and knead it for 10 minutes (see opposite). Then, put it into a clean bowl.

5. Cover the bowl with plastic foodwrap. Leave it in a warm place for 1½ hours, until the dough rises to twice its original size.

These rolls were sprinkled with poppy, sesame or sunflower seeds, or rolled oats, after they were brushed with milk.

Grease the baking tray with oil.

6. Put the dough back on the floury surface and knead it again, for about a minute, to squeeze out any air bubbles.

7. Break the dough into 12 pieces. Roll them into balls and put them on a greased baking tray, with spaces between them.

8. Leave the rolls to rise in a warm place for about 40 minutes. Heat your oven to 220°C, 425°F, gas mark 7.

9. Lightly brush the rolls with milk. Bake them for 12-15 minutes, then lift them out and put them on a wire rack to cool.

Kneading

Herby rolls

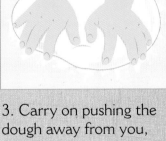

1. Press the heels of both hands, or your knuckles, into the dough. Then, push the dough away from you firmly.

2. Fold the dough in half and turn it around. Push the dough away from you again. Then, fold it in half and turn it around.

3. Carry on pushing the dough away from you, folding and turning it around, until it feels smooth and springy.

For herby rolls, stir two teaspoons of mixed herbs into the flour and salt in step 1 of the main recipe. Then, follow the steps.

Creamy raspberry ice cream

This delicious ice cream contains crushed raspberries and meringues. You can either use ready-made meringues or make your own (see pages 82-83). Make the ice cream the day before you eat it, because it takes a long time to freeze.

It's not good to re-freeze ice cream when it's been out of the freezer for a while, so put it into two containers if you're not going to eat it all at once.

Ingredients:

Serves 8

225g (8oz) fresh raspberries
50g (2oz) icing sugar
150ml (¼ pint) Greek yogurt
300ml (½ pint) double or
   whipping cream
50g (2oz) meringues

1. Put the raspberries in a colander. Rinse them, then dry them with a paper towel. Put them into a bowl and mash them with a fork until they are fairly smooth.

2. Using a sieve, sift the icing sugar into the bowl. Stir it into the mashed raspberries. Then, add the yogurt to the mixture and stir everything together well.

3. Pour the cream into a large bowl. Whisk it until it is thick and there are points when you lift the whisk. Then, add the raspberry and yogurt mixture to it.

If you're eating all the ice cream at once, use one container.

4. Gently turn the mixture over and over with a spoon, to mix everything together. Then, pour it into two freezer-proof containers and put on the lids.

Decorate each serving of ice cream with a raspberry and a sprig of fresh mint.

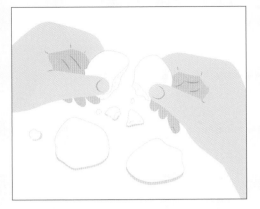
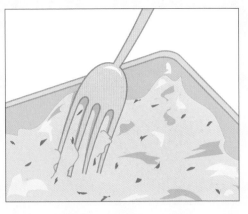
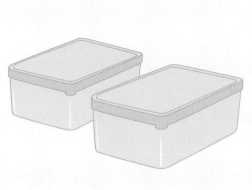

5. Put the containers into a freezer for two hours, or until the ice cream is mushy and half-frozen. Meanwhile, break the meringues into small pieces.

6. Quickly mash the ice cream with a fork, to break up any ice crystals. Then, add half of the broken meringues to each container, and stir them in.

7. Put the ice cream back into the freezer for four hours, or until it is firm. Take it out about 15 minutes before you want to eat it, so that it can soften a little.

Chef's Tip

You'll find it much easier to serve the ice cream if you use a hot spoon or ice cream scoop. Dip the spoon into a mug or bowl of hot water, dry it, then use it.

Fluffy lemon cheesecake

This light, fluffy cheesecake is easy to make and doesn't need cooking. It does need to chill in the fridge for at least four hours, though, so you'll need to make it well before you want to eat it.

Ingredients:

Serves 6

175g (6oz) digestive biscuits
75g (3oz) butter
2 lemons
2½ teaspoons powdered gelatine (not suitable for vegetarians)
225g (8oz) mascarpone, cream cheese, or another full-fat soft cheese
150ml (¼ pint) Greek-style yogurt
75g (3oz) caster sugar
150ml (¼ pint) double cream

a 20cm (8in) flan tin, or spring-clip tin with a loose base, about 5cm (2in) deep

1. Pour a little cooking oil into the tin and wipe it over the inside of the tin with a paper towel. Then, put the digestive biscuits into a clean plastic food bag.

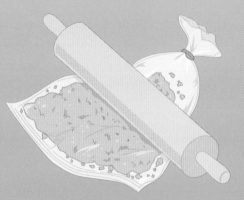

2. Put the plastic bag inside another bag and twist an elastic band around the top. Then, roll a rolling pin over the biscuits, to crush them into crumbs.

3. Put the butter into a saucepan and heat it over a low heat until it has melted. Lift the pan off the heat and stir in the biscuit crumbs. Mix them in really well.

4. Spoon the mixture into the tin and spread it out. Press it down with the back of a spoon, to make a firm, flat base. Then, put the tin in the fridge.

Cut the cheesecake into slices and decorate each slice with grated lemon rind and a strawberry.

Put the grated rind to one side.

5. Grate the rind of the lemons on the fine holes on a grater. Then, cut the lemons in half and squeeze the juice from them, using a lemon squeezer.

6. Pour five tablespoons of lemon juice and two tablespoons of cold water into a heatproof jug. Sprinkle the gelatine over the top and leave it for five minutes.

Be careful not to splash yourself with the hot water.

7. Meanwhile, fill a saucepan with water until it is about 5cm (2in) deep. Heat the water until it boils, then take it off the heat. Carefully put the jug into it.

Chef's Tip

In the next step, you need to dissolve the gelatine. Stir the liquid until the grains have dissolved, then lift up a spoonful of the liquid and check that it is clear.

Don't boil the gelatine.

8. When the gelatine has dissolved, put on oven gloves and carefully lift the jug out of the water. Leave the liquid for five minutes, to cool.

9. Put the soft cheese, yogurt, sugar and lemon rind into a bowl. Stir them hard until the mixture is smooth. Then, pour the cream into another bowl.

10. Whisk the cream firmly with a whisk until it is quite thick. Then, add the cooled gelatine to the cheese mixture and mix it in really well.

11. Add the cream. Then, gently slice through the middle of the mixture with a metal spoon and turn it over. Repeat this until everything is mixed.

Spread out the mixture with the back of a spoon.

12. Pour the mixture into the tin, then put it in the fridge for at least four hours, to set. Remove the cheesecake from the tin before serving it.

Apple crumble

This tasty apple crumble is made with eating apples and can be eaten hot or cold. It is delicious served with cream or a scoop of vanilla ice cream.

Ingredients:

Serves 4

For the crumble topping:
75g (3oz) plain white flour
75g (3oz) wholemeal flour
small pinch of ground cinnamon
100g (4oz) butter
50g (2oz) light soft brown sugar

For the apple filling:
675g (1½lb) eating apples
25g (1oz) caster sugar
3 tablespoons orange juice

Use a sieve.

1. Heat the oven to 180°C, 350°F, gas mark 4. While it is heating up, sift both kinds of flour and the cinnamon into a large bowl, to get rid of any lumps.

2. Tip any bits of bran left in the sieve into the bowl as well. Then, cut the butter into small cubes. Add the cubes to the flour mixture and stir them in.

3. Rub the butter into the flour with the tips of your fingers. Carry on until the mixture looks like fine breadcrumbs. Then, stir in the soft brown sugar.

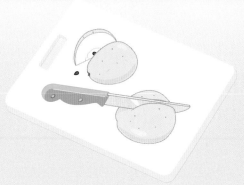

4. On a chopping board, carefully cut each apple in half. Place the halves on the chopping board with their flat side facing down, then cut them in half in again.

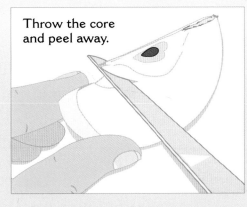

Throw the core and peel away.

5. Using a potato peeler, peel the quarters. Carefully cut the core out of each one, cutting away from you. Then, cut the quarters into small chunks.

6. Put the chunks of apple into a bowl and sprinkle the caster sugar over them. Using a spoon, mix the apple and sugar together until the apple chunks are covered in sugar.

7. Spoon the apple into a small ovenproof dish and drizzle the orange juice over the top. Spoon the crumble topping over the apple and spread it out evenly.

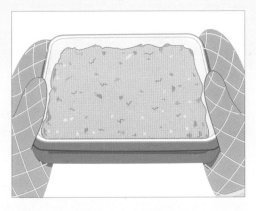

8. Put the dish onto a baking tray. Put the tray into the oven for 35 minutes, or until the top is lightly browned. Lift out the crumble and let it cool for five minutes.

Chef's Tip

When you take the crumble out of the oven, you need to check that the apple is cooked. Push the tip of a knife into it. If it isn't soft, cook it for a little longer.

Mini meringue nests

These meringue nests can be made a day or two before you want to eat them. Just keep them in an airtight container, then fill them with cream and fruit.

Ingredients:

Makes 8 meringue nests

For the meringues:
2 medium eggs, at room
   temperature
100g (4oz) caster sugar

For the filling:
150ml (¼ pint) double cream
half a teaspoon of vanilla essence
225g (8oz) berries, such as
   strawberries, raspberries
   and blueberries

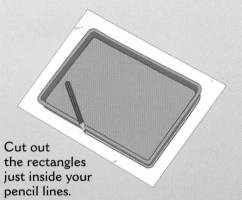

Cut out the rectangles just inside your pencil lines.

1. Heat the oven to 110°C, 225°F, gas mark ¼. Then, lay two baking trays on baking parchment. Draw around them. Cut out the shapes and lay them in the baking trays.

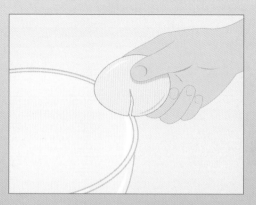

2. To separate the egg white from the yolk, break one egg on the edge of a bowl. Slide the egg slowly onto a small plate. Then, put an egg cup over the yolk.

These nests are shown slightly bigger than real size.

You don't use the yolks in this recipe.

3. Holding the egg cup, tip the plate over the bowl, so that the egg white dribbles into it. Then, do the same with the other egg, so that both whites are in the bowl.

4. Whisk the egg whites with a whisk until they are really thick. When you lift the whisk up, the egg whites should make stiff peaks, like this.

5. Add a heaped teaspoon of sugar to the egg whites. Whisk it in well. Then, keep adding spoonfuls of sugar and whisking them in, until you have added all the sugar.

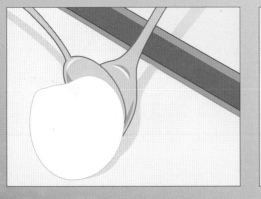

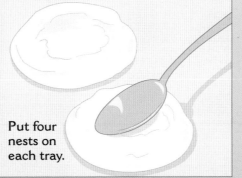

Put four nests on each tray.

The baking trays will still be hot.

6. To make the nests, scoop up a spoonful of the meringue mixture with a dessertspoon. Then, using a teaspoon, push the spoonful off onto one of the baking trays.

7. Using the back of the teaspoon, make a shallow hollow in the middle of the meringue mixture. Then, make seven more nests, leaving spaces between them.

8. Put the meringue nests in the oven. Bake them for 40 minutes, then turn off the oven, leaving them inside. After 15 minutes, carefully lift them out.

Spread the cream with a blunt knife.

9. Leave the nests on the baking trays to cool. Meanwhile, pour the cream and vanilla into a small bowl. Strongly whisk them with a whisk, until the mixture is thick.

10. Wash the berries and dry them on a paper towel. Then, when the nests are cold, fill the hollow in each one with cream and decorate them with berries.

Chocolatey baked bananas

These yummy bananas are baked in foil parcels in the oven. Eat the bananas with the hot glossy chocolate sauce drizzled over the top. They are delicious served with ice cream, too.

Ingredients:

Serves 4

25g (1oz) butter, softened
40g (1½oz) soft light brown sugar
1 teaspoon golden syrup
a small pinch of ground cinnamon
4 large, firm bananas
1 tablespoon fresh lemon juice

For the chocolate sauce:
100g (4oz) plain chocolate drops
2 tablespoons golden syrup
15g (½oz) butter
2 tablespoons water

Chef's Tip

In this recipe, you use golden syrup, which can be tricky to measure. Heat the spoon in hot water before you start, as this makes the syrup slide off easily.

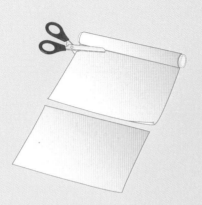

1. Heat the oven to 200°C, 400°F, gas mark 6. Then, cut four rectangles of kitchen foil for the foil parcels. They should each measure about 30 x 20cm (12 x 8in).

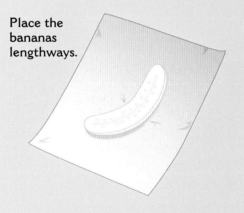

Place the bananas lengthways.

3. Peel the bananas and cut each one in half, lengthways. Rub them all over with the lemon juice. Then, place half a banana in the middle of each foil rectangle.

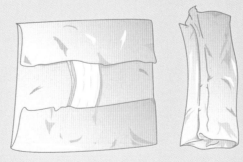

5. To make a parcel, fold the short edges of the foil over the banana. Then, pull the long edges together over the top. Squeeze the foil, to seal the parcels.

2. Put the butter in a bowl and stir it firmly with a wooden spoon until it is soft and creamy. Then, stir in the sugar, syrup and cinnamon really well, too.

4. Spoon the butter and cinnamon mixture onto the flat sides of the bananas. Then, press the other banana halves on top, to sandwich the mixture in the middle.

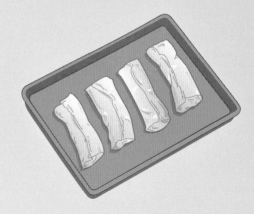

6. Put the parcels on a baking tray and bake them in the oven for 15 minutes, until the bananas are tender. While they're cooking, make the chocolate sauce.

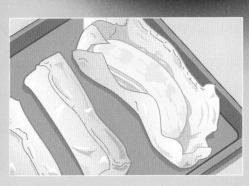

7. Put the chocolate, syrup, butter and water in a small saucepan. Heat the mixture over a low heat and stir it all the time, until it is smooth. Take the pan off the heat.

8. Remove the foil parcels from the oven and leave them for about five minutes, to cool. Carefully open the parcels, watching out for any hot steam.

9. Carefully tip each parcel, so that the bananas and sauce slide into a bowl. Then, use a smaller spoon to drizzle chocolate sauce over the bananas.

Pancakes

Pancakes are delicious with lemon juice and golden syrup, but you can also spread them with jam, honey or chocolate spread.

Ingredients:

Serves 4 (makes about 8 pancakes)

For the pancakes:
100g (4oz) plain flour
salt
1 medium egg
300ml (½ pint) milk
sunflower oil, for wiping

Suggested toppings:
lemon wedges, for squeezing
golden syrup

1. Put the flour and a pinch of salt into a sieve and sift them into a large bowl. Make a deep hollow in the middle of the flour. Then, break the egg into a cup.

2. Pour the egg into the hollow, then start to mix it with a whisk. Meanwhile, add a little milk and gradually mix the milk and egg with the flour around the hollow.

Fold the pancakes into quarters, then pile them up and drizzle them with golden syrup. Then, squeeze lemon juice over the top.

3. Add some more milk and mix it with more of the flour. Repeat this until all the ingredients are mixed together. Then, whisk the batter well, to mix in any lumps.

4. Pour a little of the oil into a cup, ready for wiping the pan. Then, heat a 20-23cm (8-9in) non-stick frying pan over a medium heat for about a minute.

5. Dip a paper towel into the oil and carefully wipe the inside of the pan with it. Be very careful that your fingers don't touch the hot pan.

The batter will bubble as it cooks.

6. Pour about half a ladleful of batter into the pan, then take the pan straight off the heat. Carefully swirl the batter around, to spread it out into a circle.

7. Put the pan back on the heat and cook the pancake for about a minute, until the top looks dry. Loosen the edges with a spatula and check that it is golden brown.

8. Slide the spatula under the pancake, then lift the pancake and turn it over. Cook it for another 30 seconds, then slide it out of the pan, onto a plate.

Chef's Tip

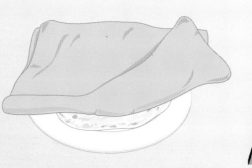

9. Cover the pancake with a clean tea towel, to keep it warm. Then, heat the pan and wipe on more oil. Make more pancakes, until all the batter is finished.

When you're making pancakes, the first one often doesn't work very well. If this happens, don't worry – throw it away and just make some more.

Strawberry shortcake

Strawberry shortcake is made up from layers of sweet scone, cream and strawberries. Put the layers together just before you eat the shortcake.

Ingredients:

Serves 8

For the shortcake:
225g (8oz) self-raising flour
1 teaspoon baking powder
50g (2oz) butter or margarine
25g (1oz) caster sugar
1 medium egg
5 tablespoons milk
half a teaspoon of vanilla essence
extra milk, for brushing

For the filling:
225g (8oz) strawberries
150ml (¼ pint) double or
  whipping cream
3 tablespoons Greek yogurt
icing sugar

Use a sieve.

1. Heat the oven to 220°C, 425°F, gas mark 7. Using a paper towel, wipe some butter over a baking tray. Then, sift the flour and baking powder into a large bowl.

2. Cut the butter into small cubes. Add the cubes to the flour, then rub them in with the tips of your fingers. Carry on until the mixture looks like fine breadcrumbs.

Decorate the top of the shortcake with half strawberries.

3. Stir in the caster sugar and make a hollow in the middle of the mixture with a spoon. Then, break the egg into a mug and stir it with a fork, to mix the white and yolk.

4. Stir the milk and vanilla into the egg, then pour the mixture into the hollow in the flour. Mix all the ingredients with a blunt knife, to make a soft dough.

5. Sprinkle a clean work surface with a little flour, then shape the dough into a ball with your hands. Squash the ball a little, then put it onto the work surface.

Remove the stalks before you slice the strawberries.

Cut the shortcake like this.

6. Using a rolling pin, roll out the dough until it is a circle which is about 20cm (8in) across. Lift it onto the baking tray and brush it with a little milk.

7. Bake the shortcake in the oven for 12-15 minutes, until it has risen and is golden brown. Meanwhile, rinse and dry the strawberries, then cut them into thick slices.

8. Take the shortcake out of the oven and slide it onto a wire rack, to cool. When the shortcake is cool, very carefully cut it in half with a bread knife.

Put the shortcake on a plate.

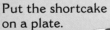

9. Lift the top layer onto a chopping board and cut it into eight wedges. Then, pour the cream into a bowl. Whisk it until it is thick, then mix in the yogurt.

10. Using a blunt knife, spread half of the mixture over the bottom half of the shortbread. Then, lay the strawberry slices all over the top of the mixture.

11. Spread the rest of the cream mixture over the strawberries. Lay the eight shortcake wedges on the top, then sift icing sugar over the top of the shortcake.

Raspberry profiteroles

These delicious pastry buns are stuffed with raspberry cream. They are best served with hot chocolate sauce poured all over them.

Ingredients:

Serves 4-6

For the pastry:
2 medium eggs
65g (2½oz) plain flour
50g (2oz) butter
150ml (¼ pint) water

For the raspberry cream:
125g (5oz) fresh raspberries
1 tablespoon caster sugar
150ml (¼ pint) double or
    whipping cream

For the chocolate sauce:
100g (4oz) plain chocolate drops
2 tablespoons golden syrup
15g (½oz) butter
2 tablespoons water

Shake off the water.

1. Heat the oven to 200°C, 400°F, gas mark 6. Using a paper towel, wipe some butter over two baking trays. Hold each baking tray under the cold tap for a few seconds.

2. Sift the flour through a sieve onto a piece of greaseproof paper. Then, break the eggs into a small bowl and beat them with a fork, to mix the whites and yolks.

You could pile all the profiteroles in a heap, before pouring on the chocolate sauce.

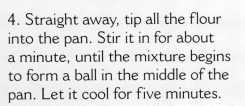

3. Cut the butter into small pieces and put it into a saucepan with the water. Heat the pan very gently over a low heat. As soon as the mixture boils, take it off the heat.

4. Straight away, tip all the flour into the pan. Stir it in for about a minute, until the mixture begins to form a ball in the middle of the pan. Let it cool for five minutes.

5. Add a little egg. Stir it in hard, then repeat this until you've added all the egg. Then, put teaspoonfuls of pastry onto the baking trays, leaving spaces in between them.

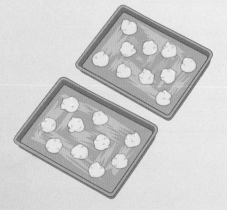

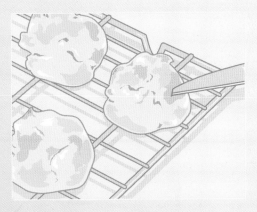

6. Bake the buns for 10 minutes, then turn up the heat to 220°C, 425°F, gas mark 7. Bake the buns for another 15-20 minutes, until they are puffy and dark golden.

7. Lift the baking trays out of the oven and put the buns onto a wire rack, using a fish slice. Then, prick a hole in the side of each one with a sharp knife, to let out any steam.

8. Put the raspberries in a colander and rinse them. Dry them with a paper towel, then put them into a bowl with the sugar. Mash them with a fork until they are smooth.

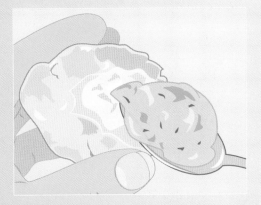

9. Pour the cream into a bowl and beat it with a whisk until it is thick and there are points when you lift the whisk. Then, add the mashed raspberries and mix them in.

10. When the buns are completely cold, cut a hole in the side of each one. Using a teaspoon, fill the hollow inside them with the raspberry cream mixture.

11. Put the profiteroles into bowls. Put them in the fridge, then make the chocolate sauce, following step 7 on page 85. Pour the sauce over the profiteroles and serve them.

Sticky chocolate cake

This sponge cake is made by mixing all the ingredients in the same bowl. It is covered in a layer of sticky chocolate icing and has some of the chocolate in the middle, too. It's delicious on its own or with cream poured over it.

Ingredients:

Makes about 8 slices

For the sticky chocolate icing:
150g (5oz) plain chocolate
150ml (¼ pint) double cream

For the chocolate sponge cake:
200g (7oz) self-raising flour
half a teaspoon of baking powder
4 tablespoons cocoa powder
4 medium eggs
225g (8oz) soft margarine
225g (8oz) light soft brown sugar
1 tablespoon milk

two 20cm (8in) round cake tins

Chef's Tip

When you're making a cake, take the eggs and margarine out of the fridge half an hour before you start cooking. This makes the ingredients easier to mix.

1. For the chocolate icing, break the chocolate into pieces. Put the pieces into a heatproof bowl and add the cream. Then, pour about 5cm (2in) water into a saucepan.

3. Let the icing cool for a few minutes. Then, put it in the fridge for at least an hour, stirring it every now and then, as it thickens. Meanwhile, make the cake.

Cut out the circles just inside your pencil lines.

5. Draw around the tins, cut out the circles and put them into the tins. Then, put the flour, baking powder and cocoa into a sieve and sift them into a large bowl.

2. Heat the water until it bubbles, then take the pan off the heat. Put the bowl into the pan and stir the chocolate and cream until the chocolate has melted.

Use a paper towel.

4. Heat the oven to 180°C, 350°F, gas mark 4. Pour a little cooking oil into each tin and wipe it over the insides. Then, put the tins on some greaseproof paper.

Stir the mixture until it is smooth.

6. Break the eggs into a mug. Add them to the large bowl, then add the margarine, sugar and milk. Stir everything well. Spoon the mixture into the tins and smooth the tops.

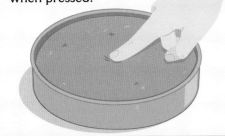

If the cakes are cooked, they will spring back when pressed.

This loosens the edges, making the cakes easier to turn out.

Use a blunt knife.

7. Bake the cakes in the oven for about 25 minutes. Then, wearing oven gloves, carefully lift them out. Press them with a finger, to see if they are cooked.

8. Leave the cakes in the tins for five minutes. Run a knife around them and turn them out onto a wire rack. Peel off the greaseproof paper and leave them to cool.

9. Spread some of the icing over the top of one of the cakes, then put the other cake on top. Then, spread the rest of the icing over the outside of the cake.

Keep the cake in a fridge until you are ready to eat it.

Useful cooking tips

There are many simple skills which cooks use all the time, but they're not all obvious when you start cooking.

On this page, there are a few tips and hints which you may find useful:

Using a food processor

Click the bowl into place.

Make sure that both parts of the lid are in place.

1. When you're using a food processor, always be very careful of the sharp blades. First, put the food into the plastic bowl.

2. Put on the main lid and twist it on firmly. Switch on the food processor and process the food for as long as you need to.

Whisking cream

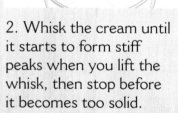

The cream gets thicker as air bubbles are whisked in.

1. Pour the cream into a bowl. Hold the bowl tightly in one hand and twist the whisk around and around very quickly.

2. Whisk the cream until it starts to form stiff peaks when you lift the whisk, then stop before it becomes too solid.

Clean bowls

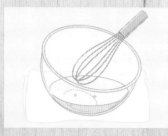

When you're whisking egg whites, use a clean, dry bowl and whisk. If you don't, the whites won't go light and fluffy.

Sticky doughs

To stop a sticky dough sticking to your hands and kitchen equipment, dust your hands and equipment with flour.

Juicing a lemon

1. If a recipe includes lemon juice, you can use bottled juice, but fresh juice is better. First, cut a lemon in half.

2. To squeeze out the juice, press one half at a time onto a lemon squeezer. Twist the lemon as you press down.

Grating cheese

1. When you grate cheese, there's always a little left over, so cut a piece which weighs more than you need.

2. Grate some of the cheese, then weigh the cheese you have grated. If there isn't enough, grate some more.

Thickening sauces

1. When you heat sauces, they get thicker, especially if there is flour in them. To avoid them sticking, stir them often.

2. To make a sauce thicker, heat it over a low heat, until it is as thick as you want it to be. Stir it all the time.

Index

The sign (*v*) after a page number means that the recipe is vegetarian.